Five Years of Crisis

by

Robert Skidelsky

the centre for
global studies

Centre for Global Studies 2013

ISBN 978-0-9546430-2-7

Contents

Preface

Six of the articles in this booklet are co-authored: No. 10 with Michael Kennedy, No. 14c with David Blanchflower, Nos. 15, 18, and 20 with Felix Martin, and No. 38 with Marcus Miller. I am grateful to them for allowing me to reproduce them here, and for sharpening up my economics.

I thank the *Sunday Times* for allowing me to reprint a letter from Professor Tim Besley and others on February 14, 2010, which started the 'war of economists', and the *New Statesman* for allowing me to reprint two articles by Vince Cable responding to my arguments.

I would also like to thank Christian Westerlind Wigstrom, Pete Mills, Nan Craig and Leanne Stickland.

With a few trivial exceptions, these articles and speeches are reproduced as they first appeared. Occasionally, I have restored cuts made by editors for reasons of space. With two exceptions, the headlines of the articles are those given them by editors.

Robert Skidelsky,
December 16, 2013

Introduction to the Second Edition – Five years of crisis

After three years of flat-lining, the British economy has started to grow again. We should all be pleased with that. What the supporters of Osborne's austerity policy are not entitled to claim is that his critics were wrong, and should hold their heads in shame.[1] As far as I know, no critic of Osbornism claimed the British economy would never recover. All economies do, sooner or later, however big the shock. But policy makes a difference. It can influence the speed of recovery, the strength of the recovery, and the kind of recovery, all three being linked.

The critics' charge against Osborne is that fiscal austerity prolonged the recession; that prolongation of the recession has destroyed productive capacity; and that reliance on monetary rather than fiscal policy has skewed the recovery towards exactly the kind of 'bubble' activities – house buying, financial speculation, and debt-fuelled consumption – which caused the collapse in the first place.

In short, policy has imposed very large costs in terms of growth foregone, the capacity to grow, and an unbalanced economy liable to crash again. All of this suggests that the recovery now going on is 'cyclical', not 'secular' - that the economy will oscillate round a low growth trend, significantly below its historical trend.

The question is: could better results have been achieved at less cost? This is a properly economic question, but also a human one. Supporters of austerity show little feeling for the many millions who were made to suffer years of *extra* unemployment, under-employment, and falling real incomes for the sake of austerity. They are doubly victims: first of the imprudence of the banks, then of the miserliness of the Chancellor.

Looking back over five years it is interesting to see how the argument for austerity shifted. At first in 2010 there was a widespread belief in official circles in something called 'expansionary fiscal contraction' – the idea that cutting the deficit would in and of itself produce recovery because of the confidence it engendered. A lot of critics' time was wasted in countering this, their position being that the reduction in demand would swamp any effect on confidence. This has now been accepted, and no one talks of 'expansionary fiscal contraction' any longer.

1   E.g. David Smith, economics editor of the Sunday Times, Sunday Times 8 December 2013.

Around the same time, the Chancellor and his supporters argued that it was necessary to cut the deficit, whatever its real effects, to counter the threat of a fiscal crisis and a flight from sterling. 'If we don't act now', went the argument, 'we will go the way of Greece'. The critics spilled a lot of ink trying to show that this argument too was false: Britain, with its own central bank and centuries' old record of not defaulting on its public debt, was never in danger of going the way of Greece.[2]

When recovery failed to emerge from austerity, the Chancellor and his cohorts put the blame on the eurozone crisis, ignoring the fact that eurozone governments were pursuing the same policies as he was, with the same results.

Finally, in October 2011, Mr. Osborne authorised the Bank of England to initiate a second bout of quantitative easing, as a result of which an extra £175bn was poured into the economy. This was an admission that something had to be done to offset the depressing effects of fiscal policy. In conjunction with fiscal subsidies to house buying, monetary policy does seem to have produced a patchy recovery. The question of course is how long this can continue?

Critics who argued that the Chancellor would never get rid of his deficit on schedule were right. The deficit in 2013-4 will be twice what it was forecast to be in 2010, even after the latest spurt of growth. The critics' argument was straightforward: no policy which did not produce growth would solve the budgetary problem, because while the government can control its spending, its revenue depends on the size of the economy. Now we are told that another £12bn a year will have to be cut out of the welfare bill to meet the zero deficit goal in 2017-8[3]. To which the question is: from where does the Chancellor expect the necessary growth over the next five years to meet his revised targets to come from?

Keynes wrote in 1936: 'Speculators may do no harm as bubbles on a steady stream of enterprise. But the position is serious when enterprise becomes the bubble on a whirlpool of speculation. When the capital development of a country becomes a by-product of the activities of a casino, the job is likely to be ill-done'.

It is the 'steady stream of enterprise' we lack. Workers have been experiencing falling real wages since 2009 and this is expected to continue halfway through next year. After a sharp fall, consumption is

2   The best Ken Rogoff could do was to come up with the British default to the USA on its First World War debt, the last of the debtors so to do. (See Skidelsky, article 44 in this book)
3   Chris Giles (December 12, 2013) "George Osborne outlines plan for more welfare cuts", Financial Times

now growing, but much of it is driven by a rundown in savings rather than higher incomes. Business investment remains a shocking 26 per cent below its pre-crisis peak at the beginning of 2008[4].The banking system is still risk-averse, and the Chancellor, while exhorting it to lend more, piles new regulations on it which will reduce its incentive to lend.

Growth may strengthen sufficiently in the next two years to win the Coalition a second term. But for those more interested in getting the arguments than the politics right, the experiment is not over. In *human* terms it was never worth putting the British economy through the wringer for three years. I still believe that, as a result of this, the recovery will be feebler and end in another crash before we get back to anything like full employment. However, if the rebound proves to be strong and sustained then one might just be able to argue that *economically* it was worth it.

Robert Skidelsky
16 December 2013

---

4   OBR (December 2013), "Economic and fiscal outlook", p70-71

Introduction

This is a selection of my writings and speeches on the Great Contraction, which started in 2008 and is set to continue. It has been the biggest global economic collapse since the Great Depression of 1929-1932. In the autumn of 2008, my agent, Michael Sissons, suggested that I write a book about it. This appeared in June 2009 under the title of Keynes: The Return of the Master. (A revised paperback followed a year later.) So I have been thinking and writing about the economic debacle pretty continuously throughout the years covered by this volume.

The reader will quickly gather that my perspective on these events is Keynesian. When the abridgment of my three-volume life of John Maynard Keynes was published in 2003, I thought I finished with Keynes. I had spent over twenty years of my life on him, and looked forward to doing other things. But when the banking crisis struck, to almost universal amazement and incomprehension, I felt it my duty to return to the fray. Keynes had insisted on the inherent instability of an unmanaged market system, and for thirty years after his death in 1946 we lived in a system of managed capitalism, which delivered historically unprecedented high and stable growth rates. However, from the 1970s onwards the tools of economic management had been discarded, one by one, in homage to a revived belief in the superior wisdom of the market. Economic performance worsened on almost all indicators. When nemesis struck in 2008, politicians, bankers, Treasury officials, analysts, and soothsayers found themselves bereft of relevant theory, because the reigning doctrines discounted the possibility of any such catastrophe occurring. The public too was bewildered and easy prey to moralistic slogans: universal impoverishment was the price people had to pay for universal greed; belt-tightening was the only way back to health. I felt I had to bring Keynes back into the picture.

These essays and speeches are my attempt to do so. I believe that the reason we are not yet out of the woods, more than three years after the crisis struck, is because Western governments have been pursuing the wrong policies. They prematurely abandoned the 'stimulus' measures to which the scale of the collapse briefly drove them, and reverted to traditional, pre-Keynesian policies of fiscal austerity. Since the autumn of 2009 they have, at the urging, and with the imprimatur, of official bodies like the IMF and OECD, committed themselves to time-tabled programmes of deficit-reduction, mainly by cutting public spending.

In the face of a similar policy response in the 1930s, Keynes introduced the supremely valuable idea of the 'fallacy of composition'. Behaviour, he argued, which is perfectly rational for the individual in isolation can be economically destructive if pursued by everyone. A key application of this idea is the 'paradox of thrift'. If every household and firm, whether from lack of confidence, or excessive debt, is trying to increase its own saving, the result will be a rundown in national income, output, and employment. If, in these circumstances, the government, too, tries to 'save' more, by cutting down its own spending, this will make things even worse. Eventually the economy will come to rest in a state of stable equilibrium well below its potential of production.

To avoid this outcome the government should increase, not reduce its spending – in practice add to its deficit – so as to offset the decline of private spending. The fact that governments instead joined the private sector in the drive for 'retrenchment' explains why the feeble recovery of 2010 has petered out, and contraction is set to resume.

This is the burden of most of the pieces in this book. Like Keynes's own *Essays in Persuasion*, they may strike the reader as the 'croakings of a Cassandra'. I am not claiming that they stand comparison with those superb essays of 1931, either in style or content. One difference is decisive: Keynes was working out his own ideas from scratch, while modern Keynesians have the benefit of Keynesian theory. So his thoughts were original, whereas mine are mere applications of his. Where our efforts at persuasion become similar is that Keynesian theory has been almost entirely obliterated from public discourse, so I often felt as though I was saying something totally unfamiliar. In the policy debates since 2008 Keynesians have been an embattled minority. Paul Krugman, Bradford De Long, Nouriel Roubini, Joseph Stiglitz, and Larry Summers in the United States, Danny Blanchflower, Samuel Brittan, Larry Elliott, Will Hutton, William Keegan, Marcus Miller, Martin Wolf, Adam Posen, and myself in the UK have been more or less consistent expansionists against the far more numerous and influential body of haverers and cutters. Opinion is much more evenly divided in the economics profession, but most academic economists have not joined the public debate – either through unwillingness, or because they have not been able to get their views into the media. So the public discussion of policy bears an uncanny resemblance to that of the early 1930s.

Keynes pointed out that behind the orthodox 'cures' for a slump lay a theory of the economy which assumed there was no slump to cure. The same is true now. Today's crop of statesmen seem to believe that, contrary to appearances, all available resources are already in use. If they appear to be idle, this is because they are not available. So the unemployed are not available for work. They have chosen leisure. I don't suppose that most politicians believe this literally. But they are slaves of ideas which cause them to behave as though they did believe it. This is what makes them so feeble in resisting the demands of the bond markets.

Anyone arguing the case against the 'cuts' is faced with two objections, which are generally deemed decisive, but which actually testify to the impoverished state of current thinking.

Defenders of austerity say: "Your policy amounts to increasing the deficit now in order for it to come down later. This is highly implausible." The reply is that the hole in the government's budget is largely – though not entirely – caused by the hole in the economy. If expanding the deficit brings into employment productive resources which the contraction has rendered idle, the deficit will automatically shrink as the economy recovers and government revenues grow. Deficit reduction should therefore not be the aim of policy; it has no intrinsic value. Rather, the government should strive for a return to higher employment and GDP. Positive growth will help reduce the deficit; zero or negative growth is bound to enlarge it. Instead of asking how increasing the deficit now will reduce it later, we should be asking how cutting expenditure is going to create growth.

The second argument adduced by the defenders of austerity goes like this: "Your case for expanding the deficit may or may not be technically correct. But the bond markets will slaughter any government that attempts it. They will notice that the national debt is rising, and seeing a risk of default, they will demand a higher price for the privilege of holding it. This will not only drive up the government's own debt-interest charges, but the whole structure of interest rates, making it increasingly costly for private businesses and households to borrow. Any extra government spending will be offset by the rise in interest rates. Only a credible programme of deficit reduction will give the investor 'confidence' that the government's debt will be honoured. This will reduce the cost of government debt, and thus reduce the interest rates charged to private borrowers."

The Chancellor, George Osborne has repeatedly averred that it is his deficit-reduction plan alone which has kept the yield on British government debt at a historic low. Had this plan not been announced, and believed, the cost of British government debt would have soared to the Greek level, and any prospect of recovery aborted.

To this the quick reply is: "The low cost of UK government borrowing is not the result of confidence in the Chancellor's deficit-reduction plan.

It is largely due to the danger of 'sovereign' debt default by Eurozone countries, and the bond markets know very well that the UK is different and will never default, because it has its own national currency, with contracts settled in sterling, and a Central Bank which can keep interest rates down by printing sterling to whatever amount necessary. The United States is in the same position. A secondary reason is that in a stagnant economy, with few prospects of capital appreciation, investors will prefer to put their money into risk-free gilts."

It has to be admitted though that the Keynesian narrative has so far failed to gain traction in the current debates. Partly this is due to the sheer scale of indebtedness, private and public, incurred both before and during the downturn, which seemed to make alternatives to orthodox finance too risky to contemplate. Beyond this, though, lies an instinctive puritanism which tends to assert itself in moments of financial panic. It is in a way natural to see our woes as the retribution for previous extravagance; and easier to believe that the only cure lies in belt-tightening than to make the effort to which Keynes summoned us to work out the consequences for economies and societies of everyone putting on the hair shirt simultaneously. However, it was the duty of the economics profession to point out the fallacies in popular reasoning, and in this task it has signally failed.

It is very difficult for me to feel confident that present policies of cutting down will lead us to recovery. Indeed, it is hard for me not to believe that matters will get worse. In the end there will be some sort of recovery whatever the government does. But it may take a long time. If my advocacy of a Keynesian theory of the economy, leading to different policies, can help shorten that interval at all, it will have done some good.

I. PROLOGUE - ON THE BRINK

The review which opens this section, written in the autumn of 2008, introduces the origins of the economic collapse of 2008. Apart from reminding readers of the details of the banking collapse of 2007-8, it points to the failure of economists – and of economics – to spot the flaws in the system of de-regulated finance. I believed, and continue to believe, that behind the mistakes of bankers, regulators, and politicians lay the failure of economic ideas, and particularly those of the Chicago School, the recently dominant school of macroeconomics. Hence the reconstruction of economics is as necessary as other more concrete reforms if we are to manage our economic affairs sensibly in the future.

1. On the threshold - of what?

Times Literary Supplement | December 26, 2008

The Trillion Dollar Meltdown: easy money, high rollers and the great credit crash
by Charles R. Morris
Public Affairs £13.99

The Credit Crunch: housing bubbles, globalization and the worldwide economic crisis
by Graham Turner
Pluto Press. Paperback. £14.99

The Conscience of a Liberal: reclaiming America from the Right
By Paul Krugman
Allen Lane. £20

Common Wealth: economics for a crowded planet
By Jeffrey Sachs
Penguin. £22

New Frontiers in Free Trade: Globalization's future and Asia's rising role
By Razeen Sally
Cato Institute. $18.95

The Economists' Voice: Top economists take on today's problems
By Joseph E. Stiglitz, Aaron S. Edlin and J. Bradford DeLong. Editors
Columbia University Press. £14.95

Of the six books under review, all published this year, only the two by non–economists, Charles R. Morris and Graham Turner, have an inkling of the economic blizzard in store. This reflects the fact that the crisis, at least in its severity, came as a complete surprise to professional economists. The Nobel laureates Paul Krugman and Joseph E. Stiglitz, represented here, have written as though the outstanding fault of the present capitalist system lies not in its instability, but in its distributional effect – both domestic and global. Even now it is not clear how far economists have started to question the economic assumptions that underlie the large–scale collapse we are living through.

Morris, an American lawyer and investment banker, seems to have anticipated the present credit crunch for some years. His book, *The Trillion Dollar Meltdown*, is the best account I have read of its genesis, written before the crunch had become global. In part, it is the story of financial innovation carried to self–destructive excess. At the same time, Morris unwittingly exposes the flaw in the financial system: it was too complicated for anyone but a professional investor to understand. This is also a problem with his book. Though it is excellently written, and full of arresting thoughts and phrases ("Intellectuals are reliable lagging indicators, near–infallible guides to what used to be true"), the world of financial legerdemain which it reveals is simply too opaque for the averagely well–educated reader to understand.

The credit crunch, originating in the American subprime mortgage crisis of 2007 and then spreading out to the global banking system, had its origins in a gigantic credit bubble. How did this arise? Morris identifies three enabling conditions. The first was the coming to power of the Chicago School of economists, with its deregulating philosophy. A key deregulating move was the repeal in 1999 of the Glass–Steagall Act of 1933, which aimed to separate retail from investment banking. "While Keynesians prayed to the idol of the quasi–omniscient technocrat, the Friedmanite religion enshrined the untrammelled workings of free market capitalism". The second condition was what he calls the "Greenspan put". Announcing a "new paradigm of active credit management", Alan Greenspan, Chairman of the Federal Reserve from 1987 to 2006, held the Federal funds rate down to 1 per cent from 2003 to 2005 as the economy went into overdrive. His message to the market was: no matter what goes wrong, the Fed will rescue you by creating enough cheap money to buy you out of your troubles. The third condition was what Morris calls a "tsunami of dollars" – the result of America's huge trade deficits, financed largely by East Asia. It was Chinese savings invested in US Treasuries which enabled Greenspan to keep the interest rate at 1 per cent for thirty months. "America's housing and debt binge was made in China."

It was in this regime of deregulated markets, cheap money and Asian–financed consumption demand that leveraged (debt–dependent) finance took off. The stages in the rake's progress were the junk bond explosion of the 1980s, the development of mortgage–backed securities or "pass throughs", the creation of portfolio insurance to "manage" the extra risk, and the sprouting of hedge funds to buy up the riskiest debt and sell it to wealthy speculators. Credit agencies fed the bubble by giving bonds containing "toxic waste" triple–A ratings. Morris does not decry the value of all this financial engineering. But the new investment instruments, while hugely enlarging credit facilities by spreading risk, suffered from dangerous flaws only revealed in moments of stress. A small number of institutions – global banks, investment banks, hedge funds – built an unstable tower of debt on a tiny base of real assets. So long as a cheap–money regime forestalled defaults, the tower might wobble but stay erect. A rise in interest rates from 2005 onwards brought it crashing down. Morris comments tartly: "Very big, very complex, very opaque structures built on extremely rickety foundations are a recipe for collapse". His forecast of a "true shock–and–awe surge of asset write downs through most of 2008" proved to be all too accurate.

What needs to be done? The key requirement is to restore effective oversight of the financial services industry. Morris makes the excellent point that banks make high profits by taking large risks, but their losses are partly socialized. Banks cannot be both public utilities and risk–taking institutions. If the taxpayer is to be liable for losses, through deposit insurance or bail–outs, then risk–taking by banks must be severely limited. This points towards restoring some version of the old Glass–Steagall Act.

Morris's book provokes an obvious reflection. The financial system should never be allowed to take on a life of its own. It provides a service to the public and should never be beyond the understanding of the public or at least of those who regulate it on the public's behalf. In other words, it should be simple to understand. Banks should be banks, not speculators: insurance companies should insure real assets; prudential rules should limit debt–to–equity ratios. There would then be less demand for the service of high–powered mathematicians to invent instruments which bamboozle the rest of us. Yes, there will be less credit available, conceivably a slower rate of economic growth. But most people will feel more secure, less stressed, and more in control of the machine that disposes of their future.

The economic consultant Graham Turner may also claim to have read the runes. *The Credit Crunch: Housing bubbles, globalization and the worldwide economic crisis* fills an important gap in Morris's story, by relating recent credit bubbles to the changing structure of the real economy. We often forget that since the financial system was deregulated in the 1980s, we have had nine major financial collapses in different parts of the world, plus major stock exchange collapses. Turner's thesis, in brief, is that globalization has resulted in a global shift in world GDP shares from wages to profits. The result has been a crisis of "realization" – over–investment in relation to worker demand. In the face of wage stagnation in the United States, American consumption demand could be kept going only by the expansion of debt. In other words, if you are a worker you don't get your productivity gains but are encouraged to borrow. The housing bubbles in the West were deliberately created to mask the damage inflicted by American companies transferring jobs to China and East Asia to boost profits. Western governments acquiesced in job exports because this fitted their strategy of promoting free trade. The real requirement is to rebalance power in the American economy between "omnipotent capital and weak labour". This rebalancing requires, among other things, protection of American jobs.

It is good to see the venerable under–consumptionist story wheeled out to explain the present credit crunch. There is a problem, though, which Paul Krugman points out in *The Conscience of a Liberal: Reclaiming America from the Right*: the numbers don't add up. True enough, "income inequality is as high as it was in the 1920s". But this is not due to globalization. Globalization might explain the rising gap between skilled and unskilled workers. It does not explain the gains of the super–rich, the main winners of recent years. In the 1970s CEOs at 102 major companies were paid $1.2 million on average in today's money. This was only a bit more than in the 1930s and only forty times that of the pay of the average full–time worker. By the early 2000s CEOs in the same companies were paid over $9 million a year, 367 times the pay of the average worker, whose benefits, additionally, had been greatly reduced. The explanation for this "great decompression", as Krugman calls it, lies in politics. From the 1980s, American politics was captured by "a vast right wing conspiracy" which set about dismantling the protective structures of the New Deal by creating "distractions". The chief of these was race. Race, in particular, duped the white voter into neglecting his material interests. Race is the main explanation for America's lack of universal health–care: whites did not want integrated hospitals. But Krugman is hopeful that the neoconservative domination is coming to an end. The last part of the book explains his plan for creating "guaranteed universal health care" for all Americans.

Krugman provides a brisk romp through twentieth–century American history from a Democratic point of view. As he tells it, this history traces two great arcs. The first, political economy arc is from high inequality in the "gilded age" – the late nineteenth century to the 1920s – to relative equality in the middle years, and back again from Ronald Reagan onwards. The second, political arc parallels it from extreme polarization to bipartisanship and back. The reality of the first arc is readily attested by the statistics of income distribution, though Krugman provides no real explanation for these swings: why, for example, did arguments for financial deregulation and lower taxation gain such traction in the 1980s, having earlier been successfully resisted? However, the political arc doesn't do the work Krugman wants it to. It is true that American politics became polarized again the 1980s, after a period of bipartisanship. But any change of governing philosophy is likely to start life as partisan. Krugman forgets that FDR's New Deal was highly divisive too. Nor is there anything bipartisan about

Krugman's own history. The Republicans, in his view, were acceptable when they acted like Democrats; when they did not, they were trying to roll back the twentieth century.

What Krugman offers is a social democratic account of history's trajectory, which is occasionally derailed by the antediluvian forces of fundamentalist religion and racist bigotry. But any historian knows that material progress is not history's only storyline, and that religious and tribal feelings are not just "distractions" from humanity's rational goals, but are as constitutive of human nature as is the desire for "more for less". There was an ideological, programmatic aspect to Democratic politics in the 1960s which Krugman intermittently acknowledges – indeed he espouses it today – but which plays no part in his explanation of why the bipartisanship of the mid century broke up. He conveniently forgets that the Democrats excoriated the complacent Eisenhower years which he now loves. A combination of Barack Obama and the excesses of neo–conservative economics will probably give America the chance to "complete the New Deal". But Krugman should remember that it was the limitations of the first New Deal that made it acceptable to Republican America.

Jeffrey Sachs's *Common Wealth: Economics for a crowded planet* is also a cry for action. Its main idea is that human activity has now become so extensive that it has thrown every life–sustaining system on the planet out of kilter. If Sachs is troubled by the thought that humanity is on the wrong treadmill, he does not allow it to cloud his optimism. He comes to the reader not as a philosopher, but as a doctor offering readily available cures for the main planetary diseases he diagnoses: human pressure on the ecosystem leading to dangerous climate change, population pressure on scarce resources, and the extreme poverty of one–sixth of the world's population. With only a modest investment, we can achieve sustainable development, stabilize the world's population at 8 billion (it is now 6.6 billion), and end extreme poverty. All "we" need is the necessary political will.

Sachs displays a disappointingly uncritical attitude towards the science he adduces in support of his plans. To some extent he is the victim of his own multidisciplinary approach. Working at the Earth Institute at Columbia University has been to him an "unalloyed gift". And his range of knowledge is impressive. But he inevitably has to take a huge amount on trust, and it shows. This is not a book of scholarship but an executive summary of hundreds of reports of blue ribbon commissions, research papers, convergences and UN declarations. The bullet points roll off the assembly line of his prose, with scarcely a hint of doubts, still less self–doubt.

Sachs presents himself as an economist of the toolkit, but in fact, he is a moralist who believes it his mission to save the planet. With such an attitude, it is almost impossible for the scientist not to become a preacher. Like his fellow moralist Paul Krugman. Sachs presents a one–sided dossier in support of his cause. A reader who knows at least something about the subjects being discussed, without fully sharing the passion of the author, is bound to deplore his lack of attention to opposing arguments, whether on climate change, population or the utility of aid for economic development.

Sachs's uncritical attitude to science is matched by his naivety about politics. He seems to believe that the main reason for government failure to tackle global problems with the required vigour is organization deficiencies (for example, failure to mobilize available knowledge), forgetting that governments – and more generally politics – have not been set up to solve global problems but to protect their countries against domestic disorder and external attack. While berating Western governments for their failure to shape up to their planetary tasks, he pays surprisingly little attention to what it is now usual to call the problem of "governance" in the poorest countries. African countries fail to live up to their "convergence potential" because they lack basic levels of infrastructure, health, education "and governance". But for many development economists, "governance" is not something to be added to a list of infrastructural projects financed by the World Bank. It is what makes such projects possible. And the quality of "governance" is embedded in the habits and customs of the people. Sachs never faces up to the issue of how much "governance" will have to be imported from elsewhere to realize the millennium goal of poverty elimination, or how this is to be done.

Global networks, he thinks, may be the answer. "A wonderful new project, e–Parliament", he enthuses, "aims to knit together the world's parliaments and assemblies by video conferencing and the Internet to forge a new kind of hybrid democratic institution at the transnational and even global scale". National Parliaments could mobilize the best brains through simultaneous teleconferences. He ends up by proposing a billionaires' foundation to eradicate world poverty. I have no doubt that it will be established. No one else need apply for the post of director.

Despite the book's deficiencies, Sachs's main thrust is convincing: the problems he identifies can be solved, by the methods he outlines. His fault is that he is much too impatient and optimistic. Societies progress at their own pace. They can be tweaked a little by scientists. More likely, they will be jolted out of stagnation by disaster. There will be many of those to come, and many regressions as well, before Sachs's dreams are realized. It is naive to imagine that it can be otherwise.

Razeen Sally is a wide–ranging historian of economic thought, and his clearly written monograph *New Frontiers in Free Trade* has been heavily influenced by his studies in the Scottish Enlightenment foundations of classical liberalism. He is an unqualified advocate of free trade and globalization, but points out that, historically, free trade was only one element in the Victorian political–economy package, which included domestic laissez–faire, low balanced budgets, and the gold standard. The international liberal order of the nineteenth century was not constructed by international organizations, but emerged as a by–product of acts of domestic liberalization. This unity between external and domestic liberalism broke down after 1945 when "[Adam] Smith abroad" had to be reconciled with "Keynes at home". The post–1945 theory of commercial policy developed by James Meade, Harry Johnson and Jagdish Bhagwati uncoupled free trade from laissez–faire by advocating targeted subsidies instead of protection for infant industries. The case for free trade came to be argued in purely technical terms. But social democracy at home was ideologically inconsistent with free trade abroad. This made free trade vulnerable to attacks by anti–globalizers.

The lesson that Sally draws from all this is that globalization today should be pursued by unilateral action rather than by complicated multilateral negotiations through the World Trade Organization. Attempts to secure common minimum standards as a condition for lowering trade barriers will lead to regulatory overload. Pressures to harmonize labour, environmental, food–safety, and other product standards will have a chilling effect on labour–intensive exports. An increasingly politicized WTO will have to bear the brunt of the anti–globalization backlash and NGO pressure. Sally points out that in Asia, unilateral dismantling of trade barriers has been the rule, with China as its driving force. This challenges the consensus that trade liberalization must be based on reciprocity. Welfare gains result directly from import liberalization, regardless of anyone else's concession. The WTO could be retained as a useful auxiliary to "national market–based reforms".

Sally's case for unilateral liberalization – for instance, dismantling American and EU farm subsidies without waiting for another trade round – is persuasive, but it has little chance of gaining a hearing in the West today. The problem, which he admits, is that globalization threatens the living standards not just of unskilled and skilled workers, but of the Western middle class as a whole. "The political challenge", he writes, "is to keep borders open and extend market–based reforms, while containing inevitable protectionist pressures". But he does not tell us how this is to be done.

In *The Economists' Voice: Top economists take on today's problems*, "more than thirty of the world's top economists offer innovative policy ideas and insightful commentary on our most pressing economics issues". The book is divided into nine sections ranging from climate change – now the obligatory problem number one – to the pros and cons of the death penalty. Each section consists of two or more short non–technical essays, helpfully prefaced by a summary of the essays it contains. Although three essays warn of the coming collapse of the housing bubble, there is no sense of the scale of the impending crisis. For example, Robert Schiller writes that while homeowners face a "substantial risk of much lower prices", fortunately "derivative products, notably a futures market, are being developed [so] that they will soon be able to insure against this risk".

The collection illustrates the power and limits of economics. Economics is the most inventive of the social sciences in its ability to suggest how incentives might be rearranged so as to secure desirable outcomes at least cost in money, bureaucracy and liberty. But it lacks a realistic account of politics, the arena in which what is desirable can be made to happen. Joseph Stiglitz illustrates both features in his missionary essay on climate change: "The well–being of our entire planet is at stake. We know what needs to be done. We have the tools to hand. We only need the political resolve" – which to many will mean that we don't have the tools to hand, since political resolve is a tool too, which Stiglitz doesn't tell us how to invent.

The same lack of political understanding is apparent in the discussion of the costs of the Iraq war. From the economists' point of view, the editors ask, "could not [the money] have been better spent on fighting global climate change, on providing vaccine commitments to fight tropical disease, on brokering Israeli–Palestine peace, or on giving ten million children in the United States or abroad each a $100,000 scholarship"? The answer is yes, but the economists cannot explain why these alternatives were not adopted.

The book is full of excellent cut and thrust. In his essay on international capital mobility, J. Bradford DeLong discusses how events have dented his faith in its untrammelled operation. Fifteen years ago, he supported capital mobility unreservedly. But now he believes that too many external costs are associated with financial crises. Capital also seems to want to flow, not from but to where it is already abundant – the United States has become a giant vacuum cleaner sucking in capital from all round the world – and even when efficient, capital flows benefit rich people from poor countries, not the poor. However, DeLong cannot abandon his neoliberalism; "in the end we may have to tolerate the equality–lessening reverse flow of capital in order to promote the equality–increasing and wealth–increasing diminution of corruption." At least he is honest enough to admit the dilemma.

The cumulative impression left by these six books is that we are on the cusp of one of those periodic changes in political economy caused by a crisis of the existing order. The end of the liberal/social democratic era lauded by Paul Krugman was brought about by the crisis of inflation and permissiveness. The succeeding neoconservative era supported by Razeen Sally is likely to end in a crisis of financial excess. Keynesianism and socialism, only recently proclaimed dead, are risen from their graves. The last Soviet leader, Mikhail Gorbachev, recently remarked that, what with all the bail–outs of banks and corporations going on, we now seem to have capitalism for the poor and Communism for the rich. This is a neat easy way of saying that we stand on the threshold of uncharted territory.

II. WHY KEYNES?

These three pieces are a distillation of my understanding of John Maynard Keynes, drawn from my three-volume of my biography of the economist (abridged as *John Maynard Keynes: Economist, Philosopher, Statesman*, 2003) and my short book, *Keynes the Return of the Master*, published in 2009.

Keynes often used the words 'cash' and 'liquidity' interchangeably. The important idea, though, is liquidity, not cash. A liquid asset is one that can be used or sold quickly without loss of value. Cash (especially under the bed) is the main example of such an asset in normal times, but so is a government bond. So a 'flight to liquidity' denotes a flight from equities to cash and bonds. It is associated with growing uncertainty: the less you know about future expenditure the more cash you need under the bed to cover potential outlays.

2. An impossible crash brought Keynes back to life
The Times | October 23, 2008

When Alistair Darling said that "much of what Keynes wrote still makes sense", anyone under 40 might well have asked: "And who on earth is Keynes"?

When I first started writing about him in the early 1970s, John Maynard Keynes was a name to conjure with - not in the league of Led Zeppelin, to be sure, but certainly familiar to the mythical educated layman. Economic policy was "Keynesian" - that is, governments aimed to keep unemployment below the "magic" figure of one million, as they had for the previous 30 years, by varying public spending and taxes.

Then Keynesian policy suddenly became obsolete and the theory that backed it was consigned to history's dustbin. He might have been a great economist, right for his times - the Great Depression of the 1930s - but he had nothing to offer the modern world, and moreover was responsible for the "stagflation" of the 1970s. In her assault on inflation, Margaret Thatcher put the Keynesian engines into reverse and created three million unemployed. Keynes seemed as dead as the dodo.

In fact, while dead to the public, Keynes lived a ghostly half-life in the corridors of the Bank of England and the Treasury. In setting interest rates, the Bank continued to pay attention to what was happening to output as well as inflation - although the inflation rate was its only "target". Gordon Brown's fiscal rules allowed for the influence of the "automatic stabilisers": the movement of the budget into deficit or surplus as the economy slowed or speeded up.

But basically the authorities relied on "managing expectations", by the gentlest adjustments to interest rates, to keep us in perpetual non-inflationary boom; we lived in a world from which inflations and depressions had been banished, and for which Keynes was no longer needed.

For ten years the new formula worked. We were blessed with what Mervyn King, the Governor of the Bank of England, called a "nice" environment – a combination of strong growth in the US and Far East and the downward pressure on prices of a competitive globalising economy. More fundamentally, Keynesian economics was rejected by most of the economic profession as having caused inflation in the 1970s.

The main prescription of the "new" classical economics was to minimise the role of government and let markets do their job. It rested on an assumption that if economic agents are rational – the key assumption on which the claim of economics to be a science is based –

the market system accurately prices all trades at each moment in time. If this is so, boom-bust cycles must be caused by outside "shocks" – wars, revolutions, above all political interference with the delicate adjustment mechanisms of the "invisible hand" of the market.

But this view has been blown sky-high by the present crisis. For this crisis was generated by the market system itself, not some outside "shock"; moreover, within a system that had been extensively deregulated in line with mainstream teaching. The automatically self-correcting market system to which the economics profession has mostly paid homage has been shown to be violently unstable. And this is exactly how Keynes expected it to behave.

What was left out of the mainstream economics of his day, and its "post-Keynes" successor, was the acknowledgement of radical uncertainty. "The outstanding fact," Keynes wrote in his magnum opus, *The General Theory of Employment, Interest and Money* (1936) "is the extreme precariousness of the basis of knowledge on which our estimates of prospective yield have to be made". We disguise this uncertainty by resorting to a variety of "pretty, polite techniques", of which economics is one, "which try to deal with the present by abstracting from the fact that we know very little about the future".

But any view of the future based on "so flimsy a foundation" is liable to alternating waves of irrational exuberance and blind panic. When panic sets in there is a flight into cash. But while this may be rational for the individual, it is disastrous for the economy. If everyone wants cash, no one will lend. As Keynes tellingly reminded us "there is no such thing as liquidity... for the community as a whole". And that means that there may be no automatic barrier to the slide into depression, unless a government intervenes to offset extreme reluctance to lend by huge injections of cash into the banking system.

This is exactly what world governments have been doing, in defiance of the contemporary theory that tells them that the huge mispricing of debt which provoked the present meltdown is impossible.

What the Chancellor rightly pointed out is that the rescue of the banking system may not be enough to avert a deep recession, and a fiscal stimulus may be needed. The International Monetary Fund is predicting that output will fall short of trend by 1.05 per cent of GDP this year, rising to 3.16 per cent next year. With unchanged policy, the result may well be three million unemployed in two years' time. Yes, the economy will ultimately correct itself without government stimulants. But it may take a long time, with huge damage while the required "corrections" are taking place. This is the case for a Keynesian rescue operation.

Beyond the ambulance work, there is the question of working out a policy framework, domestic and international, that will at least minimise the danger of these self-destructive market-generated storms arising in future. Politics, of course, will compel all kinds of new regulations, good and bad, to rein in the wild excesses of recent times.

But politics is blind: the politicians are like passengers on the Titanic rushing to the lifeboats. But unless their policies are backed by a more adequate theory of economic behaviour than is currently available they will not survive when times return to "normal". Keynes tried to supply that theory. He may not have clinched his case, but even his arch-critic Milton Friedman conceded that it was "the right kind of theory" for his times. Because the possibility of collapse is always present, Keynesian theory remains a better guide to policy than one that assumes that markets are inherently stable.

Keynes understood that it is ultimately theory that determines policy, and that one cannot for a long time justify policies that run counter to accepted theory. He also said: "In the long run we are all dead." That is one observation which happily does not apply to him. Over to you, Darling.

3. What would Keynes have done?

The Independent ∣ November 22, 2008

Expect plans for higher borrowing, tax cuts, and more spending in Monday's pre-Budget statement. With Britain sliding into depression, it is not surprising that the old Keynesian tool kit is being ransacked. But Keynesian economics is not just about fixing damaged economies. You don't need very sophisticated economics to spend your way out of a depression. In one form or other – usually by war or war preparations – governments have been doing this throughout history.

It does require very sophisticated economics to prove that depressions cannot happen. This was the economics Keynes set out to challenge in his great book, *The General Theory Of Employment, Interest And Money*, written during the Great Depression of the 1930s. His own ideas, he wrote, were "extremely simple, and should be obvious". Economies were inherently unstable; governments had a vital role to play in stabilising them.

These heresies were too simple and obvious for the economics profession. For after a long and rather successful trial run, Keynesian economics was obliterated by the free-market revolution which swept the Anglo-American world under Thatcher and Reagan. In a notable comeback, updated versions of the theory Keynes had challenged "proved" that unregulated or lightly regulated market economics were very stable, and that government interventions only made things worse. But in apparent disregard for mathematical demonstrations to the contrary, crises and crashes, booms and busts continued to occur, and politicians continued to try to mitigate their consequences, their common sense being stronger than their logic. This is roughly the situation we are in today. Economic theory points to non-intervention: politics points to intervention. Keynes's attempt to marry the two in the notion of "practical statecraft" failed.

Keynes's "simple and obvious" ideas can be summed up in two propositions. The first is that large parts of the future are unknowable. The "unknowability" of the future imparted an inherent instability to financial and investment markets, leading to periodic outbreaks of "herd behaviour", when "new fears and hopes will without warning take charge of human affairs".

Economics "abstracted" from uncertainty, by assuming, Keynes wrote, that uncertainty could be "reduced" to calculable probability, and therefore to the same status as certainty itself. This underlies today's "efficient market hypothesis" which treats uncertainty as measurable risk; its acceptance explains the explosion of the derivatives market since the 1980s, which has brought the financial system crashing down.

Keynes's second proposition is that depressions can last a long time, longer than it is politically safe to tolerate. He did not doubt that markets worked "in the long run". "But this long run," he wrote in his best-known remark, "is a misleading guide to current affairs. In the long run we are all dead."

Keynes offered a number of reasons why economies did not simply "bounce back" after a great shock (the Dow Jones index did not recover its 1929 prices till 1952). However, his clinching argument in his 1930s debates with free market economists such as Friedrich Hayek was political. It was much too risky to allow economies to slide into deep depression. The example of Hitler was vivid in the minds of all democratic politicians. In 1928, at the height of Weimar Germany's prosperity, the Nazis got 2 per cent of the vote. By 1930 they were up to 18 per cent. In 1933 Hitler was in power.

During that time, German unemployment had risen from two million to six million. Hayek and the free market economists never had an answer to this political argument. So what should the British Government do now? In 1931 Keynes favoured the devaluation of sterling, but this is now irrelevant: the pound is not fixed to gold as it was in his day, and is sinking quite naturally. The suggestion most favoured by editorial columns is to cut interest rates and go on cutting them. Keynes was certainly not against this, but "cheap money" to counter depression is not specifically Keynesian, and he doubted the efficacy of monetary policy on its own.

The Bank of England might flood the banks with money, but this would not necessarily produce greater lending if the tendency to hoard money was going up at the same time. "The possession of actual money," Keynes wrote, "lulls our disquietude; and the premium which we require to make us part with money is the measure of the degree of our disquietude." As the adage has it: you can bring a horse to water but you can't make it drink.

This leaves fiscal policy as the unique instrument in the Keynesian tool kit. It is idle to speculate whether Keynes would have favoured tax cuts or public spending increases. His remedies were always tailored to their impact on the state of confidence. His essential point was that, in a depression, a government stimulus was needed to offset the decline in private spending. This would mean running a temporary budget deficit. If pessimistic analysts are right in predicting a shrinking of GDP next year in the order of 3 to 4 per cent, the increase in the current deficit might have to be very large, even larger than the 2 per cent Vince Cable is proposing.

With output and inflation falling, Keynes would not have worried about the "dangers of inflation". "The boom, not the slump," he wrote in 1937, "is the right time for austerity at the Treasury."

The final question is this. Will we be content simply to take Keynes out of his cupboard from time to time, dust him down, and put him in charge of rescue operations, before putting him back firmly in his cupboard? Or will we now try to run our affairs paying proper attention to his insights into financial instability so as to prevent these alternations of mania and panic from periodically seizing control of our lives?

4. The Remedist

New York Times | December 12, 2008

Among the most astonishing statements to be made by any policymaker in recent years was Alan Greenspan's admission this autumn that the regime of deregulation he oversaw as chairman of the Federal Reserve was based on a "flaw": he had overestimated the ability of a free market to self-correct and had missed the self-destructive power of deregulated mortgage lending. The "whole intellectual edifice," he said, "collapsed in the summer of last year."

What was this "intellectual edifice"? As so often with policymakers, you need to tease out their beliefs from their policies. Greenspan must have believed something like the "efficient-market hypothesis," which holds that financial markets always price assets correctly. Given that markets are efficient, they would need only the lightest regulation. Government officials who control the money supply have only one task — to keep prices roughly stable.

I don't suppose that Greenspan actually bought this story literally, since experience of repeated financial crises too obviously contradicted it. It was, after all, only a model. But he must have believed something sufficiently like it to have supported extensive financial deregulation and to have kept interest rates low in the period when the housing bubble was growing. This was the intellectual edifice, of both theory and policy, which has just been blown sky high. As George Soros rightly pointed out, "The salient feature of the current financial crisis is that it was not caused by some external shock like OPEC raising the price of oil. . . . The crisis was generated by the financial system itself."

This is where the great economist John Maynard Keynes (1883-1946) comes in. Today, Keynes is justly enjoying a comeback. For the same "intellectual edifice" that Greenspan said has now collapsed was what supported the *laissez-faire* policies Keynes attacked in his times. Then, as now, economists believed that all uncertainty could be reduced to measurable risk. So asset prices always reflected fundamentals, and unregulated markets would in general be very stable.

By contrast, Keynes created an economics whose starting point was that not all future events could be reduced to measurable risk. There was a residue of genuine uncertainty, and this made disaster an ever-present possibility, not a once-in-a-lifetime "shock." Investment was more an act of faith than a scientific calculation of probabilities. And in this fact lay the possibility of huge systemic mistakes.

The basic question Keynes asked was: How do rational people behave under conditions of uncertainty? The answer he gave was profound and extends far beyond economics. People fall back on "conventions," which give them the assurance that they are doing the right thing. The chief of these are the assumptions that the future will be like the past (witness all the financial models that assumed housing prices wouldn't fall) and that current prices correctly sum up "future prospects." Above all, we run with the crowd. A master of aphorism, Keynes wrote that a "sound banker" is one who, "when he is ruined, is ruined in a conventional and orthodox way." (Today, you might add a further convention — the belief that mathematics can conjure certainty out of uncertainty.)

But any view of the future based on what Keynes called "so flimsy a foundation" is liable to "sudden and violent changes" when the news changes. Investors do not process new information efficiently because they don't know which information is relevant. Conventional behaviour easily turns into herd behaviour. Financial markets are punctuated by alternating currents of euphoria and panic.

Keynes's prescriptions were guided by his conception of money, which plays a disturbing role in his economics. Most economists have seen money simply as a means of payment, an improvement on barter. Keynes emphasized its role as a "store of value." Why, he asked, should anyone outside a lunatic asylum wish to "hold" money? The answer he gave was that "holding" money was a way of postponing transactions. The "desire to hold money as a store of wealth is a barometer of the degree of our distrust of our own calculations and conventions concerning the future. . . . The possession of actual money lulls our disquietude; and the premium we require to make us part with money is a measure of the degree of our disquietude." The same reliance on "conventional" thinking that leads investors to spend profligately at certain times leads them to be highly cautious at others. Even a relatively weak dollar may, at moments of high uncertainty, seem more "secure" than any other asset, as we are currently seeing.

It is this flight into cash that makes interest-rate policy such an uncertain agent of recovery. If the managers of banks and companies hold pessimistic views about the future, they will raise the price they charge for "giving up liquidity," even though the central bank might be pumping out cash. That is why Keynes did not think that cutting the central bank's interest rate would necessarily — and certainly not quickly — lower the interest rates charged on loans. This was his main argument for the use of fiscal stimulus to fight a depression. There was only one sure way to get an increase in spending in the face of an extreme private-sector reluctance to spend, and that was for the government to spend the money itself. Spend on pyramids, spend on hospitals, but spend it must.

This, in a nutshell, was Keynes's economics. His purpose, as he saw it, was not to destroy capitalism but to save it from itself. He thought that the work of rescue had to start with economic theory itself. Now that Greenspan's intellectual edifice has collapsed, the moment has come to build a new structure on the foundations that Keynes laid.

III. AUSTERITY VS. STIMULUS

I first became concretely involved in the policy debate with my article in the *Sunday Telegraph* of 20 September 2009. This 'guest' space was allowed me by courtesy of its regular columnist, Liam Halligan, all the more generously since Liam pursued an opposite track, warning of the dangers of inflation. The Labour government was still in power and had not yet announced its medium-term budget strategy, but I see I had already singled out George Osborne as my main target. Re-reading it I see I failed to make sufficiently clear the distinction between *printing* money and *spending* money. The phrase 'injecting money into the economy' confuses the two.

The second item recalls the 'battle of economists' which started in a letter to the *Sunday Times* on 14 February 2010 by Tim Besley and nineteen colleagues calling for the government to eliminate the 'structural' deficit (an uncertain quantity which depends on estimates of the 'output gap') in a single parliament. I organised a reply, signed by a hundred economists which appeared in the *Financial Times* on 18 February. I am now much more sceptical about the size, or even existence, of a "structural deficit" than I was then.

The article I wrote with Michael Kennedy, 'Future Generations will Curse Us' (*Financial Times* 27 July 2010) made the crucial distinction between capital spending and current spending, which became the basis for my subsequent calls for a National Investment Bank.

I reproduce a sequence of three articles in the *New Statesman*, which started with one by me on 25 October 2010, followed by one by Vince Cable, the Business Secretary, on 12 January 2011, which was partly a reply to mine, which in turn elicited a reply to Mr. Cable by Danny Blanchflower and myself on 24 January 2011. This was, I believe, the only occasion when a government minister has been prepared to debate publicly with the critics of government economic policy.

5. George Osborne fails to mind the output gap
Sunday Telegraph | September 20, 2009

It was John Maynard Keynes who first pointed out the importance of the "output gap", and its consequences for policy. Keynes said that policies which are sound and necessary when the economy is fully employed, are unsound and destructive when the economy is shrinking.

He knew what he was talking about. He had lived through the Great Depression of 1929-32 when governments did what they were supposed to do in normal times: balance the budget and hold fast to sound money. The result was the greatest economic disaster in modern history – one matched only by the political disaster which followed in its wake.

Keynes's crucial distinction between full employment and subnormal employment was totally ignored by George Osborne in his speech "The Conservative Strategy for Recovery" last week. At no point in his speech did Osborne mention that UK output has fallen by 5 per cent since last October and unemployment has risen by over one million. The gap between what we can produce and what we do produce has grown to more than £70bn. This is because, as a nation, we are spending £70bn less.

Almost all that Osborne said is right and sensible in conditions of full employment; most of it is wrong and wrong-headed when there is heavy and persisting unemployment. Although he understands that we have been in the deepest recession since the war, his strategy for recovery assumes that there is nothing to recover from – except a Labour government!

His sole policy to counter recession is low interest rates to reduce "our enormous private and public debt burden". Low interest rates require "tight fiscal policy". Tight fiscal policy requires cutting government spending .

What is the argument? Osborne is right to say that low interest rates are necessary to fight a recession. But they are not enough. They reduce the burden of existing debt; but, even when combined with the recapitalisation of zombie banks and guarantees on old debt, they may not lower the cost of borrowing enough to stimulate new investment.

For the volume of investment depends not just on the cost of borrowing but on the expectation of profit. Recessions are the result of a collapse in profit expectations. And it may be that no feasible reduction in interest rates can revive profit expectations sufficiently to produce a robust recovery.

Today depressive forces are rampant both on the lending and borrowing sides. Commercial banks have seized the opportunity offered by the lower Bank of England rate to rebuild their balance sheets by increasing the margins on their own lending. Since October last year profit margins measured as the spread between the swap rate and the mortgage rate have more than tripled. The volume of private investment has also shrunk. Not only has it decreased in absolute terms by almost £60bn but, crucially, by 2010 we are projected to invest 25 per cent less than before the crisis relative to GDP. We're investing a smaller portion of a diminishing cake.

This is the context in which a fiscal stimulus – deliberately increasing the size of the budget deficit – becomes not just relevant but necessary. Osborne's main argument is that Britain couldn't, and can't, "afford" a fiscal stimulus because the Government's finances were already deranged before the recession started.

Criticism of Gordon Brown's handling of the public finances in his ten years as Chancellor is certainly valid: like home owners who banked on the prices of their properties going up forever, he banked on permanent boom to keep his budgets in balance and, like them, was caught short when the boom collapsed. But Labour's fiscal record from 1997-2007 has no bearing on the question of what we can "afford" today. We couldn't afford not to have had a stimulus in the past year and we can't afford not to continue with it now.

The reason is quite straightforward. If output is falling, the Government's revenues fall automatically and its social spending rises automatically. If the Government tries to reduce the deficit by cutting its spending, it reduces total spending in the economy still further. This causes the recession to deepen and makes the deficit even larger. It is like a cat chasing its own tail.

In these circumstances a discretionary increase in the deficit – the deliberate injection of extra spending power into the economy large enough to reverse the fall in output – is the best way of reducing the deficit in the medium term. The logic of this seems to have escaped Osborne.

He is on sounder ground in criticising some of the actual measures taken. The temporary cut in VAT was useless. Further, some forms of fiscal stimulus, like spending on infrastructure programmes, take a long time to work their way into the economy. But this is an argument for a quicker-acting stimulus, not for no stimulus.

Had the Government given every household a spending voucher of £500 last Christmas, we would be facing a much smaller prospective budget deficit today.

The idea that, in present conditions, a rising budget deficit is bound to drive up long-term interest rates is moonshine. Increased household spending, diffused through the economy, would multiply the volume of bank deposits, which would have the effect of reducing the rates banks charge on loans. So a policy of expanding the budget deficit is perfectly consistent with low interest rates when private spending is severely depressed.

The Osborne effect – to coin a phrase – would occur only if there is a fixed money supply. Then, it is true that if the Government borrows more money from the public the banks will have less to lend the public. However, the Bank of England can always create the money for additional government spending by printing more money This is the meaning and purpose of "quantitative easing" – to enable interest rates to stay low even as the Government is increasing its own spending, and thus avoid "financial crowding out".

At full employment, "printing money" is the royal and pretty immediate road to runaway inflation. But when there is heavy unemployment the injection of additional money into the economy will arrest the economic slide and bring about a recovery in output and employment. This will increase the resources available to the banks for lending, and enable the Bank of England to reverse the "quantitative easing" in due course.

The dodgiest part of Osborne's argument is that "fiscal tightening" (during a recession) does not reduce output because "what you lose in government spending, you gain in exports". But you gain in exports only if the exchange rate depreciates. Osborne does not explain why "fiscal tightening" should cause the pound to sink against other currencies (the usual argument is that it is fiscal loosening which has this effect), and he does not begin to consider how far, in the absence of a stimulus, the pound would have to depreciate to plug the output gap. To fill a 6 per cent output gap with increased revenues from exports, British net exports would have to grow by about 25 per cent.

Between January 2007 and December 2008 the trade-weighted value of the pound depreciated by 27 per cent. In the same time exports only grew by 13 per cent. By this reasoning, and keeping everything else constant, the pound would have to lose another 50 per cent against its major trade partner currencies for exports to fill the output gap. In fact, the pound has recovered by 7 per cent since January 2009.

All the arguments for a stimulus go into reverse when the economy ceases to need stimulating.

Then, as Osborne rightly says, fiscal responsibility is the condition of low interest rates. And it is more than just a party point to say that Labour mismanaged the national finances before the recession, and that as a result the "size of the fiscal adjustment" needed to get the budget under control will be greater than it need have been. But as a guide for what needs doing now his analysis is way off target. By contrast, the TUC general secretary Brendan Barber was spot on when he told the Congress at Liverpool that to "try and cut a deficit during a recession and you make it worse... But in the medium and long term it must start to come down. And that is going to mean some hard choices."

6a. Letter to Sunday Times: UK economy cries out for credible rescue plan

The Sunday Times | February 14, 2010

Sir,

It is now clear that the UK economy entered the recession with a large structural budget deficit. As a result the UK's budget deficit is now the largest in our peacetime history and among the largest in the developed world.

In these circumstances a credible medium-term fiscal consolidation plan would make a sustainable recovery more likely.

In the absence of a credible plan, there is a risk that a loss of confidence in the UK's economic policy framework will contribute to higher long-term interest rates and/or currency instability, which could undermine the recovery.

In order to minimise this risk and support a sustainable recovery, the next government should set out a detailed plan to reduce the structural budget deficit more quickly than set out in the 2009 pre-budget report.

The exact timing of measures should be sensitive to developments in the economy, particularly the fragility of the recovery. However, in order to be credible, the government's goal should be to eliminate the structural current budget deficit over the course of a parliament, and there is a compelling case, all else being equal, for the first measures beginning to take effect in the 2010-11 fiscal year.

The bulk of this fiscal consolidation should be borne by reductions in government spending, but that process should be mindful of its impact on society's more vulnerable groups. Tax increases should be broad-based and minimise damaging increases in marginal tax rates on employment and investment.

In order to restore trust in the fiscal framework, the government should also introduce more independence into the generation of fiscal forecasts and the scrutiny of the government's performance against its stated fiscal goals.

Tim Besley, Sir Howard Davies, Charles Goodhart, Albert Marcet, Christopher Pissarides and Danny Quah, London School of Economics;
Meghnad Desai and Andrew Turnbull, House of Lords;
Orazio Attanasio and Costas Meghir, University College London;
Sir John Vickers, Oxford University;
John Muellbauer, Nuffield College, Oxford;

David Newbery and Hashem Pesaran, Cambridge University;
Ken Rogoff, Harvard University;
Thomas Sargent, New York University;
Anne Sibert, Birkbeck College, University of London;
Michael Wickens, University of York and Cardiff Business School;
Roger Bootle, Capital Economics;
Bridget Rosewell, GLA and Volterra Consulting

6b. Letter to the Financial Times: First priority must be to restore robust growth

Financial Times | February 18, 2010

Sir,

In their letter to the *Sunday Times* of February 14, Professor Tim Besley and 19 co-signatories called for an accelerated programme of fiscal consolidation. We believe they are wrong.

There is no disagreement that fiscal consolidation will be necessary to put UK public finances back on a sustainable basis. But the timing of the measures should depend on the strength of the recovery. The Treasury has committed itself to more than halving the budget deficit by 2013-14, with most of the consolidation taking place when recovery is firmly established. In urging a faster pace of deficit reduction to reassure the financial markets, the signatories of the *Sunday Times* letter implicitly accept as binding the views of the same financial markets whose mistakes precipitated the crisis in the first place!

They seek to frighten us with the present level of the deficit but mention neither the automatic reduction that will be achieved as and when growth is resumed nor the effects of growth on investor confidence. How do the letter's signatories imagine foreign creditors will react if implementing fierce spending cuts tips the economy back into recession? To ask – as they do – for independent appraisal of fiscal policy forecasts is sensible. But for the good of the British people – and for fiscal sustainability – the first priority must be to restore robust economic growth. The wealth of the nation lies in what its citizens can produce.

Lord Skidelsky, Emeritus Professor of Political Economy, University of Warwick, UK
Marcus Miller, Professor of Economics, University of Warwick, UK
David Blanchflower, Bruce V. Rauner Professor of Economics, Dartmouth College, US and University of Stirling, UK
Kern Alexander, Professor of Law and Economics, University of Zurich, Switzerland
Martyn Andrews, Professor of Econometrics, University of Manchester, UK
David Bell, Professor of Economics, University of Stirling, UK
William Brown, Montague Burton Professor of Industrial Relations, University of Cambridge, UK
Mustafa Caglayan, Professor of Economics, University of Sheffield, UK

Victoria Chick, Emeritus Professor of Economics, University College London, UK

Christopher Cramer, Professor of Economics, SOAS, London, UK

Paul De Grauwe, Professor of Economics, K. U. Leuven, Belgium

Brad DeLong, Professor of Economics, U.C. Berkeley, US

Marina Della Giusta, Senior Lecturer in Economics, University of Reading, UK

Andy Dickerson, Professor in Economics, University of Sheffield, UK

John Driffill, Professor of Economics, Birkbeck College London, UK

Ciaran Driver, Professor of Economics, Imperial College London, UK

Sheila Dow, Emeritus Professor of Economics, University of Stirling, UK

Chris Edwards, Senior Fellow, Economics, University of East Anglia, UK

Peter Elias, Professor of Economics, University of Warwick, UK

Bob Elliot, Professor of Economics, University of Aberdeen, UK

Jean-Paul Fitoussi, Professor of Economics, Sciences-po, Paris, France

Giuseppe Fontana, Professor of Monetary Economics, University of Leeds, UK

Richard Freeman, Herbert Ascherman Chair in Economics, Harvard University, US

Francis Green, Professor of Economics, University of Kent, UK

G.C. Harcourt, Emeritus Reader, University of Cambridge, and Professor Emeritus, University of Adelaide, Australia

Peter Hammond, Marie Curie Professor, Department of Economics, University of Warwick, UK

Mark Hayes, Fellow in Economics, University of Cambridge, UK

David Held, Graham Wallas Professor of Political Science, LSE, UK

Jerome de Henau, Lecturer in Economics, Open University, UK

Susan Himmelweit, Professor of Economics, Open University, UK

Geoffrey Hodgson, Research Professor of Business Studies, University of Hertfordshire, UK

Jane Humphries, Professor of Economic History, University of Oxford, UK

Grazia Ietto-Gillies, Emeritus Professor of Economics, London South Bank University, UK

George Irvin, Professor of Economics, SOAS London, UK

Geraint Johnes, Professor of Economics and Dean of Graduate Studies, Lancaster University, UK

Mary Kaldor, Professor of Global Governance, LSE, UK

Alan Kirman, Professor Emeritus Universite Paul Cezanne, Ecole des Hautes Etudes en Sciences Sociales, Institut Universitaire de France

Dennis Leech, Professor of Economics, Warwick University, UK

Robert MacCulloch, Professor of Economics, Imperial College London, UK

Stephen Machin, Professor of Economics, University College London, UK

George Magnus, Senior Economic Adviser to UBS Investment Bank

Alan Manning, Professor of Economics, LSE, UK

Ron Martin, Professor of Economic Geography, University of Cambridge, UK

Simon Mohun, Professor of Political Economy, QML, UK

Phil Murphy, Professor of Economics, University of Swansea, UK

Robin Naylor, Professor of Economics, University of Warwick, UK

Alberto Paloni, Senior Lecturer in Economics, University of Glasgow, UK

Rick van der Ploeg, Professor of Economics, University of Oxford, UK

Lord Peston, Emeritus Professor of Economics, QML, London, UK

Robert Rowthorn, Emeritus Professor of Economics, University of Cambridge, UK

Malcolm Sawyer, Professor of Economics, University of Leeds, UK

Richard Smith, Professor of Econometric Theory and Economic Statistics, University of Cambridge, UK

Frances Stewart, Professor of Development Economics, University of Oxford, UK

Joseph Stiglitz, University Professor, Columbia University, US

Andrew Trigg, Senior Lecturer in Economics, Open University, UK

John Van Reenen, Professor of Economics, LSE, UK

Roberto Veneziani, Senior Lecturer in Economics, QML, UK

John Weeks, Professor Emeritus Professor of Economics, SOAS, London, UK

7. Deficit Disorder: The Keynes Solution
New Statesman | May 17, 2010

The new chancellor will find himself in the worst starting position of anyone new in that job since the Second World War. According to the Treasury, we are just starting to limp out of the "most severe and synchronised downturn since the Great Depression in the 1930s". Recovery is not secure. With the Greek crisis as the trigger, the world monetary system is starting to disintegrate. The historically minded will recall that the international financial crisis of 1931, two years after the start of the Depression, aborted an incipient recovery and forced Britain off the gold standard. A double-dip recession is a distinct possibility.

Once a new government is in place, the chancellor will have to face the situation as it is, not as his party claimed it would have been had it been in power. The government's finances are dire. The £163.4bn that the Labour government borrowed in the fiscal year 2009-2010, representing 11.6 per cent of GDP, is the biggest deficit in the postwar period. Public-sector net debt at the end of March was at £890bn, or 62 per cent of GDP - an increase of almost 10 percentage points over last year.

The worsening of the public finances is mainly the result of the deterioration in the economy. This has two aspects. The British economy is 5.4 per cent smaller than it was two years ago. But in addition, the fiscal forecasts at that time assumed that the economy would continue to grow to trend, reckoned to be 2.5 per cent a year - a growth that failed to occur. As a result, the British economy is 8.2 per cent smaller than it would have been had it continued to grow at that trend over the past two years. This, and not the actual shrinkage of the economy, measures the true deterioration in economic performance and the potential deterioration in the public finances. Perhaps the forecasts were over-optimistic. But hindsight is the easiest form of virtue.

Such poor private-sector performance has inevitably had severe effects on the public finances. Tax revenues dwindle and social expenditure goes up. Of the total deficit of 11.6 per cent of GDP, 70 per cent is "structural", representing a continuation of pre-recession spending. The £14.4bn tab for the fiscal stimulus in 2009-2010, plus the "automatic stabilisers" representing increased spending on the unemployed, amount to almost 5 per cent. This spending will shrink automatically as the economy recovers: the government saves £1bn a year until 2012 for every 200,000 people who leave claimant count unemployment. The most recent projections for this year's deficit are already £13bn, lower than projections for the same period made 18 months ago.

However, even if the economy now resumes "growing to trend" - the 2010 Budget projects steady GDP growth in the next few years reaching between 3.25 per cent and 3.75 per cent in 2012, while inflation is expected to converge on the target rate of 2 per cent - there will remain a "structural" deficit of between 7 per cent and 8 per cent of GDP, which will have to be filled by increases in taxes and cuts in expenditure. The Labour government promised to launch a programme next April aimed at cutting the deficit to £74bn or 4 per cent of GDP by fiscal year 2014-2015. The Tories promised to start cutting sooner and more, but how much sooner and how much more would depend on George Osborne's promised emergency Budget.

If the recovery falters, even this drastic fiscal consolidation plan will seem inadequate. Although the stock market has recovered, the "real" economy is still struggling. In the first quarter of this year, GDP increased by only 0.2 per cent (half the figure in the last quarter of 2009), hardly the catch-up recovery some were hoping for. In February, unemployment figures rose by 43,000 to 2.5 million in total - or 8 per cent of the workforce. The US has started to grow more strongly, but Europe is flat. And, as already remarked, there is a not negligible risk of a double-dip recession.

Stimulating facts

In the pre-election period, there was a "war of economists" (see p.40-3 above), in which I myself took part.

To the outsider, the engagement might have seemed to be on too narrow a front to be interesting. It was about how soon fiscal consolidation should start. However, behind this technical issue lay two contrasting theories, or models, of the economy. The first, which we may call "classical", is highly sceptical about fiscal stimulus under any conditions. The argument is that when the government issues bonds or debt to pay for its spending, this is bound to be at the expense of private lending and borrowing. The stimulatory effect of a government deficit is therefore bound to be zero, or very small.

The second, or Keynesian, view is that this is not true when there is a lot of slack in the economy. The reason for the slack is that the private sector is not spending enough to employ all those seeking work - whether because investment prospects are too uncertain, or because it is paying off debt. In these circumstances government spending is not at the expense of private spending: it compensates for its absence. If the government were to economise on its own spending at the same time as the private sector was spending less, the result would be a slide into even greater recession. Keynes called this the "paradox of thrift".

Those in the first camp do not deny the need for some stimulus when the economy is depressed, but they think this should not be at the expense of existing private spending. The only type of stimulus that meets this requirement is printing extra money. "Monetarists" put their faith in so-called quantitative easing (QE); Keynesians are happy with printing money, but deny that it is enough. The extra money has to be spent, and only the government can ensure that it is. (There is another way: the government can give all households time-limited spending vouchers - that is, special pounds, perhaps printed red, valid only for three months, and to be spent on buying British goods - and could issue successive tranches of these until the economy revives. This move would bypass the frozen banking system, but no political party has advocated it, and we can be sure that the incoming chancellor will put the horrendous thought to one side.)

The monetarists believe that the level of aggregate income increases proportionally to the amount of extra cash made available to the banks by the Bank of England. However, Keynesians argue that the demand for cash balances varies with the state of confidence. In the old days people would start hoarding gold when confidence fell. Now they add to their cash reserves or buy liquid securities. Building up cash or liquidity buffers, however, means that the new QE money is not spent, and therefore does not contribute to increasing output. While the Keynesians accept that an increase in the supply of cash is a necessary condition for an increase in national income, they deny that it is a sufficient condition. With increased preference for liquidity, the injection of cash into the banking system by the Bank of England may not lower the rate of interest sufficiently to restore a full-employment level of aggregate spending. As Keynes put it, if money is the drink that stimulates the system to activity, "there may be several slips between the cup and the lip".

The numbers bear this out. From early 2009, the Bank of England started printing money with which to buy back government debt held by banks and non-banks. Over the year, roughly £200bn - or 15 per cent of GDP - worth of gilts and bonds was exchanged for cash. The monetarists expected a cash injection of that size into the banking system would allow Britain to leave the recession with a bang.

Yet, as the 0.2 per cent GDP growth in the first quarter of this year is telling us, there was very little bang for quite a lot of buck. So what happened? Already at the first evaluation of the QE policy in August, six months into the programme, the Treasury and the Bank had noticed that something was not working. By then £144bn had been injected, yet UK bank lending had not picked up. Money from bond sales remained stuck in the banking system. The commercial banks held on to the cash, either in the form of reserves at the Bank of England or by using it to buy new gilts or corporate bonds. Overall, in the 11 months between the launch of quantitative easing and its suspension, broad money supply (which includes bank deposits) actually fell by almost 10 per cent. And if we consider what John Slater calls "effective money" - a measure that, by including credit in the shadow banking system, is broader still - this fall is likely to have been even steeper.

The injection of money may have caused a stock-market boom in the financial economy, but on the real economy - the target of the policy - it had little effect. In short, damaged expectations may cause the credit crunch to outlast the circumstances that gave rise to it.

In such circumstances government spending needs to be the main agent of recovery - and that means fiscal policy, however it is financed. We learn from experience nonetheless. If flooding the banking system with money doesn't do the trick, there is a big problem with fiscal policy as well. The nature of this first emerged in an enthralling exchange between Keynes and the Treasury official Richard Hopkins before the Macmillan committee on finance and industry in 1930. Keynes was arguing for a big expansion of the public works programme; Hopkins countered that the effects of any government programme would depend on its effects on business confidence.

Fear of Labour

Hopkins did not disagree that government work programmes could, in principle, cure unemployment, but went on, "if you had to get [the loan] taken up at a very high rate of interest and accompanied by an adverse public sentiment you would very quickly lose what you gained by that from the number of people who would think it better to invest the next lot of money they had in America". In other words, "psychological crowding-out" would cause the government to have to pay more for its debt. Extra government spending would cure unemployment only if it did not spook the markets.

Keynes himself was fully alert to the importance of confidence. He acknowledged that "economic prosperity is excessively dependent on a political and social atmosphere which is congenial to the average businessman. If the fear of a Labour government or a New Deal depresses enterprise, this need not be the result either of a reasonable calculation or of a plot with political intent; it is the mere consequence of upsetting the delicate balance of spontaneous optimism." He would even accept a "conservative Budget . . . if this would be helpful as a transitional measure".

Keynes wrote his *General Theory of Employment, Interest and Money* (1936) not just to change the minds of economists, but to persuade the business world that government intervention to rescue failing economies would be in its interest. But he tended to the view that the root of "lack of confidence" was lack of demand for goods and services and that confidence would automatically revive with the revival of spending, however engineered. In all this, he underestimated the visceral business hatred of big government. By 1939, however, even he had come to doubt whether a "democracy would ever have the courage to make the grand experiment necessary to prove my case outside the conditions of war".

In fact, that grand experiment has never been made outside war or other than under a totalitarian state, in the sense of Keynesian policy being used to rescue an economy from a slump. Franklin D Roosevelt's "New Deal" gave Americans hope and important reforms, but achieved only a modest recovery from the Depression - largely, Keynes thought, because the scale of government spending was insufficient. Full employment in democracies was restored only in the Second World War, when the government started spending 70 per cent of the national income, with the national debt rising above 200 per cent.

The one experiment that did prove Keynes's case was undertaken in Hitler's Germany, under the aegis of the Führer's economics minister Hjalmar Schacht, though not in conditions that encouraged democratic emulation. The Schachtian system consisted of three main elements: a) controls on capital exports, b) bilateral payments agreements, whereby Germany's trading partners were only allowed to sell as much to Germany as they bought from Germany, and c) huge state credits to German industry ("printing money"), which over four years reduced unemployment from six million to near zero, with inflationary pressure being repressed by wage and price controls.

Gilt trip

Given the potentially conflicting requirements of "confidence" that he will face, what should the incoming chancellor do? He should choose the path dictated by economic reason, refuse to be spooked by what Samuel Brittan calls the "teenage scribblers", and continue to pump money into the economy, counting on this advantage: that the markets do not expect the UK government to go bankrupt.

While Greece is paying close to 11 per cent for its ten-year bonds, the UK Treasury is still paying less than 4 per cent, and the UK coupon is not even 100 basis points higher than the German. In fact, the bid yield on the ten-year gilt is roughly 50 basis points lower now than at the start of September 2008. Unless and until confidence runs out, running a Budget deficit is far less costly than a return to recession. If we fear market reactions to sluggish growth and large deficits, imagine market reactions to no growth and much larger deficits.

To ensure that the policy of continued macroeconomic stimulus does not lead to the capital strike that Richard Hopkins feared and his modern successors predict, the chancellor should be prepared to announce sharp fiscal cuts if the government's credit rating comes into serious doubt; he should promise to withdraw support for QE in the quarter that annualised inflation exceeds, say, 3 per cent; and he should promise to reconsider any type of stimulus measure once annualised GDP growth exceeds, say, 2.5 per cent for two quarters in a row. These promises could be part of a new fiscal constitution, adherence to which would be independently monitored. Spelling out precise conditions for the continuation of the fiscal stimulus would reassure the markets and shorten the period necessary to have one.

Beyond this, we cannot continue to run an economic system in which there is such a large gap between the beliefs of ordinary people and the beliefs of the business and financial worlds about the properties of the economy and the requirements of a decent economic life. Keynes rightly thought that ordinary people are instinctively more reasonable economists than economists and financiers. It is to them that the chancellor is ultimately responsible.

8. Once Again We Must Ask: "Who Governs?"
Financial Times | June 16, 2010

In 1974, Edward Heath asked: "Who governs – government or trade unions?" Five years later British voters delivered a final verdict by electing Margaret Thatcher. The equivalent today would be: "Who governs – government or financial markets?" No clear answer has yet been given, but the question may well define the political battleground for the next five years.

In one sense, next week's emergency Budget is simply the logical working out of an intellectual theorem. The implicit premise of the coming retrenchment is that market economies are always at, or rapidly return to, full employment. It follows that a stimulus, whether fiscal or monetary, cannot improve on the existing situation. All that increased government spending does is to withdraw money from the private sector; all that printing money does is to cause inflation.

These propositions are a re-run of the famous "Treasury view" of 1929. By contrast, Keynes argued that demand can fall short of supply, and that when this happened, government vice turned into virtue. In a slump, governments should increase, not reduce, their deficits to make up for the deficit in private spending. Any attempt by government to increase its saving (in other words, to balance its budget) would only worsen the slump. This was his "paradox of thrift". The current stampede to thrift shows that the re-conversion to Keynes in the wake of the financial collapse of 2008 was only skin-deep: the first story remains deeply lodged in the minds of economists and politicians.

But this story alone does not explain the conversion to austerity. Politicians clamouring for cuts in public spending do not cite Chicago economists. They talk about the need to restore "confidence in the markets". The argument here is that deficits do positive harm by destroying business confidence. This collapse of confidence may come in several forms – fear of higher taxes, fear of default, fear of inflation. Deficits thus delay the natural (and rapid) recovery of the economy. If markets have come to the view that deficits are harmful, they must be appeased, even if they are wrong. What market participants believe to be the case becomes the case, not because their beliefs are true, but because they act on their beliefs, true or false.

The parallel with what happened in 1931 is irresistible. In February of that year, Philip Snowden, the Labour government's chancellor of the exchequer, set up the May Committee to recommend cuts in public spending. The committee projected a budget deficit of £120m, later raised to £170m, the latter figure amounting to about 5 per cent of gross domestic product, and proposed raising taxes and reducing spending to "balance the budget". The international financial crisis caused by the collapse of the Austrian Credit-Anstalt bank in July 1931 brought huge pressure on the government to act on the May Report. In a notable display of patriotic fervour, the financial and political establishment united to demand cuts in unemployment benefits to "save the pound".

Keynes was one of the very few who stood out against the herd. Of the May Report's authors, he wrote: "I suppose that they are such very plain men that the advantages of not spending money seem obvious to them." They had ignored the fact that their proposed cuts would add 250,000-400,000 to the unemployed and diminish tax receipts. "At the present time," Keynes continued, "all governments have large deficits. They are nature's remedy for preventing business losses from being ... so great as to bring production altogether to a standstill."

When the Conservative-Liberal coalition that had succeeded the Labour government introduced an emergency budget in September 1931, Keynes again stood out against the chorus of approval. The budget was, he wrote, "replete with folly and injustice". He explained to an American correspondent that "every person in this country of super-asinine propensities, everyone who hates social progress and loves deflation, feels that his hour has come and triumphantly announces how, by refraining from every form of economic activity, we can all become prosperous again."

Conservative spokesmen often claim that fiscal consolidation causes economies to recover. If so, the effect of the outbreak of public frugality in 1931 was curiously roundabout. Cuts in salaries produced a "mutiny" of naval ratings at Invergordon, suggesting that the empire was crumbling. This was enough to force Britain off the gold standard. A combination of sterling depreciation and lower interest rates revived exports and started a housing boom. But there was never a complete recovery until the war. Such evidence for the success of the cuts is the stuff of castles in the sky.

We are about to embark on a momentous experiment to discover which of the two stories about the economy is true. If, in fact, fiscal consolidation proves to be the royal road to recovery and fast growth then we might as well bury Keynes once and for all. If however, the financial markets and their political fuglemen turn out to be as "super-asinine" as Keynes thought they were, then the challenge that financial power poses to good government has to be squarely faced.

9. By George, he hasn't got it: What would JM Keynes think of George Osborne's Budget?

The Independent | June 25, 2010

I don't wish to examine the structure of George Osborne's emergency Budget, but to analyse its logic. On the structure I have only this to say: the balance between increased taxes and reduced spending is probably right. It is right to demand sacrifices from all sections of the community, though I doubt the attack on welfare benefits (designed to save £11bn a year by 2014-15) will be seen by many as fair. And there are a number of useful measures to encourage enterprise. My objection is to its overall fiscal – and ideological – stance. It is deflationary – not as deflationary as the Chancellor's rhetoric demanded – but deflationary all the same.

At a time when the UK economy has an estimated "output gap" – the gap between what the economy is producing and what it has the potential to produce – of between 4 and 6 per cent (the Government's figures), I do not believe the Government should take money out of the economy; it should pump it in. I don't understand how you help growth by reducing spending.

First, a short lesson in Keynesian macroeconomics. I make no apology for starting here, because what is at issue are two opposing theories, or "models" of the macroeconomy. The message of John Maynard Keynes's *General Theory of Employment, Interest and Money* (1936) comes in three parts. First, the community's level of income and output is determined by the level of aggregate demand, or purchasing power. Second, aggregate demand, especially investment demand, can fall short of potential output, so that the community's available stock of labour and plant can exceed the demand for their services. Third, this situation can continue indefinitely, or at least for a long time, in the absence of a government stimulus to replace the missing private sector demand.

Now compare what happened in 1929-1932 (the Great Depression) and what has happened since 2008 (the Great Recession). In both periods the world economy declined at the same rate for five quarters. But whereas the Great Depression economy went on declining for another seven quarters, the Great Recession economy's decline stopped after five quarters, and there has been a very modest recovery. Almost all analysts agree this was because this time, unlike in the earlier period, governments all over the world poured a huge amount of extra money into their shrinking economies. Many allowed their deficits to expand by four or five percentage points of GDP; and their central banks flooded the commercial banks with new money.

This was good old fashioned Keynesianism. In a slump, Keynes said, governments should increase, not reduce, their deficits to make up for the fall in private spending. Any attempt by government to balance its budget in a slump would only worsen the slump.

Compare this to the key sentence on the first page of HM Treasury's Budget 2010: "Reducing the deficit is a necessary precondition for sustained economic growth" – an almost exact reversal of Keynes's theory. We have to understand that the Treasury is under new management and what it believed three months ago is not necessarily what it believes today. What we do know is that its new master, George Osborne, never believed in the stimulus. For the last two years he has been calling for its elimination as quickly as possible.

What theory of the economy makes sense of Osborne's attitude? He has never allowed himself the luxury of explicitly offering a theory. But his "model" can be inferred from his pronouncements. It can be boiled down to three propositions of expanding generality: (1) in the absence of the fiscal stimulus, the economy would have rapidly recovered to full employment; (2) following a shock, economies quickly self-adjust back to full employment in the absence of counter-productive government efforts to revive them; (3) markets are optimally self-regulating in the absence of government interference. Osborne has never said any of this precisely, but his pronouncements make no sense unless he believes these things. So it is between these two views – Keynes's and Osborne's – that we are invited to choose. Let's see how far the new Treasury view endorses the Osborne view.

What the Government aims to do is to add an extra £40bn to Labour's deficit reduction plan, both by starting earlier and by cutting faster. That is, it aims to have removed, by 2014-15, £40bn a year more from the private sector than the £73bn which Labour had wanted to remove by then: a total fiscal tightening of £113bn, or two-thirds of the current deficit. This augmented degree of fiscal tightening should eliminate entirely the "structural" deficit by 2014-15, leaving only a vestigial public sector net borrowing requirement of 1.1 per cent by 2015-16. It will also cause the decline of public sector net debt from a peak of 70.3 per cent of GDP in 2013-14 to 67.4 per cent of GDP in 2015-16. In a nutshell, Osborne aims to balance the Budget by 2014-15.

Two questions arise: why does the Osborne Treasury suppose that the UK Government's deficit had reached £155bn, or 11 per cent of GDP by 2010?[5] And by what mechanisms does it suppose that

5 The difference between the £155bn. and the £113bn was supposed to be closed by the growth of the economy. £113bn was the 'structural' element of the total projected deficit of £155bn. This suggests that Labour was already running a sizeable 'structural deficit' before the collapse – one that would not be closed by the growth of the economy. However, estimates of 'structural' and 'cyclical' elements in total deficits are highly uncertain.

removing increasing amounts of money from the economy will help the recovery?

To answer the first, let's look at some more figures: between 2002-3 and 2007-8 the Government's annual deficit averaged 2.5 per cent of GDP. In 2008-9 it shot up to 6 per cent and in 2009-10 to 11 per cent. Between 2002-3 and 2007-8 the national debt rose from 32 per cent of GDP to 36 per cent, still well below 40 per cent, which Gordon Brown had laid down as the "prudent" maximum, before rising to 44 per cent in 2008-9 and 62 per cent in 2008-10. This deterioration in the national finances has been mainly caused by the decline in the economy, so the Government has been getting less revenue and is having to spend more on social benefits. One might suppose that most of it would be reversed as the economy recovers, without any change of policy.

But this is apparently not so. The Treasury now argues that its Comprehensive Spending Review of 2007 assumed "unsustainable revenue streams" based on a property boom and excess profits in the financial sector. Worse, for years, the Treasury had been overestimating the sustainability of its revenues and therefore of its spending. Or, put another way, the Treasury's pre-recession projections of taxes and spending assumed an inflation rate of 2 per cent, or nominal GDP growth of between 4 and 5 per cent. Once the recession hit and inflation started falling, nominal GDP fell faster than real GDP, leaving a larger than expected gap between revenue and spending.

What the recession did was "reveal that the public sector was living beyond its means". This is an odd way of putting it. Whenever you have an economic collapse, you are "revealed" to be living beyond your means, as the revenue side of your balance sheet falls. But does that mean you had previously been living beyond your means? Surely not. That you can't support yesterday's spending with today's income does not mean you could not do so yesterday. The only thing the slump reveals is that some event has cut your income and you need to adjust your spending. Moreover, the private sector was just as guilty of "living beyond its means", a fact conservative commentators prefer to avoid.

Was the boom the fantasy, the slump the reappearance of reality? The answer is that the boom was neither more nor less real than the slump. The idea that asset prices in the boom were too "high" presupposes that there existed a set of objectively correct prices from which boom prices deviated. But where do such objectively correct prices come from and why are they more correct in a slump than in a boom? Expectations are only wrong in retrospect. Assets are worth no more and no less than buyers are willing to pay for them – regardless of whether we are in a slump or a boom.

My second question is: how does the Government suppose that taking money out of the economy is going to help recovery? We get an initial answer on page nine of the Budget statement: the deficit reduction plan "should underpin household, business, and market confidence". Notice the "should" here. The Treasury, unlike the Chancellor, is hedging its bets.

In the "medium term", i.e. over five years, deficit reduction will: "reduce competition for funds for private sector investment..."thus lowering long-term interest rates and boosting private sector investment. This has long been the Chancellor's main argument. It is loaded with fallacies. First, it assumes there is a fixed supply of saving, so that the more saving borrowed by the Government, the less will be available to be borrowed by the private sector. This is true at full employment, but untrue when there are unemployed resources. If the economy is underemployed, an increase in the government deficit does not encroach on existing saving; it creates additional saving by raising the national income above what it would have been. This additional saving helps finance the increased borrowing.

Secondly, the "crowding out" argument assumes that interest rates adjust the supply of saving to the demand for investment: the more saving "released" for private investment, the lower long-term interest rates will be. Keynes denied that interest rates adjusted the supply of saving to the demand for investment. Rather, interest rates adjusted the supply of money to the demand for money. If the demand for money, or more generally liquidity, is going up as a result of increased uncertainty, then the interest rate will go up, whatever is happening to saving. It may even resist attempts by the Government to lower it by flooding the banks with money. This is what has been happening: banks and money markets are awash with cash, but little of it has been trickling through to the business sector. Investment has fallen by 20 per cent since the start of the recession.

The Treasury's "crowding-out" argument is bogus. Its argument about the beneficial effect of accelerated deficit reduction hinges on its effect on confidence. The proposition is that it will reduce the perceived risk of investing in Britain. This psychological boost will be sufficient to offset any negative effect of accelerated retrenchment on demand.

I would not for a moment decry the importance of psychology. We live in an uncertain world in which decisions to invest depend on subjective estimates of risk. Osborne's argument is that deficits do positive harm by destroying business confidence. Deficits thus delay the natural (and rapid) recovery of the economy from an unexpected "shock".

How far does Osborne's Treasury buy the Chancellor's argument? The answer is: by no means completely. The basis of its scepticism is reinforced by a body which Osborne set up to monitor the Treasury's projections: an independent Office for Budgetary Responsibility (OBR) chaired by former Treasury official, Sir Alan Budd.

The OBR's central economic forecast is for "the economy to rebalance, with net exports and business investment making a greater contribution to growth than in the recent past, and government spending making a negative contribution to growth as fiscal consolidation is implemented". To translate into English: tax rises and spending cuts will tend to reduce growth in the near future by reducing consumer demand, but this may be offset and even outweighed in the medium term by increased confidence. Specifically "reassuring the private sector that concrete measures have been put in place to limit the rise in government debt could prompt households and companies to reduce precautionary saving, increasing consumption and investment relative to what they would have been otherwise". The bottom line here is the conclusion that "fiscal consolidation will negatively effect the economy in the short term", but this could be offset by favourable effects on business confidence. The blow to demand is definite; the psychological offsets are hypothetical.

But the Treasury does not rely on "confidence" alone. It is also placing its hopes on the supply-side reforms of the Budget. "Measures to promote enterprise will reduce regulation and tax rates and refocus support towards infrastructure, the low carbon economy and regional development. Measures to create a fair tax system will reward work and promote economic competitiveness." These measures will promote "sustainable" growth, not the "artificial", deficit-created growth. And so they may. But they do not address what happens in the short term.

And, finally, if confidence doesn't do the trick, the Treasury looks to monetary easing to offset the effects of fiscal austerity, even though the policy of "quantitative easing" has failed so far to bring down long-term interest rates enough to stimulate private sector borrowing.

So that's the gamble on which the coalition has staked its fate, and that of the British economy. An important footnote is an exchange between President Roosevelt and Keynes in 1938. From 1933 to 1937, America had experienced four years of recovery since the Depression, with unemployment falling from 25 per cent to 14 per cent. Keynes attributed this recovery to the solution of credit and insolvency problems and easy short term money; establishment of adequate relief for the unemployed; public works and other investment programmes helped by government funds or guarantees; the surge in private investment, and the momentum of the recovery. By the time of Keynes's letter to Roosevelt on 1 February 1938, however, the American economy was experiencing a "double dip" recession: unemployment had gone up from 14 per cent to 18 per cent, industrial production had fallen by 21 per cent and real GDP by 3.5 per cent. Keynes attributed this to the premature curtailment of the public works programme, as Roosevelt tried to "balance the budget" in 1936-37. Keynes's letter marks the start of the "Keynesian" phase of the New Deal which, by 1941 had reduced unemployment by 8 percentage points.

Whose judgement – or ideology – do we trust, Keynes's or Osborne's?

10. Future generations will curse us for cutting in a slump
Robert Skidelsky and Michael Kennedy
Financial Times | July 27, 2010

In 1937 Keynes wrote: "The boom, not the slump, is the right time for austerity at the Treasury." Jean-Claude Trichet, president of the European Central Bank, disagrees. Stripped of its jargon, his argument last Friday in the *Financial Times* is that fiscal retrenchment is needed to "consolidate recovery". This has become the standard European – though not American – line. "Failure to address the deficit is the greatest danger we face," said UK Treasury minister Lord Sassoon in the House of Lords on Monday, faithfully echoing the words of his master, chancellor George Osborne. But beyond vaguely referring to the need to restore "confidence", none of the cutters can explain how reducing public spending when private spending is already depressed will "consolidate recovery".

By contrast, Keynesian theory can readily explain why it will not. The government, Keynes argued, is the only agency that can prevent total spending in the economy from falling below a full or acceptable employment level. If private spending is depressed, it can restore total spending to a reasonable level by adding to its own spending or reducing taxes.

In doing so it will be adding to a deficit that is already the result of falling tax revenues and rising benefits due to the recession. The deficit, though, has the function of sustaining the level of total spending and output in the economy.

Any attempt to reduce it before a strong momentum to private sector recovery is established will make matters worse. Once the economy has started to grow, the deficit incurred during the recession will automatically shrink to a pre-recession level. Deliberate steps to eliminate the "structural" (ie non-recession induced) deficit should be postponed until the recovery is firmly entrenched. With the budget balanced, or even in surplus, at high employment, continued growth will steadily reduce the national debt as a percentage of gross domestic product. This is what happened after the second world war.

In Keynesian theory, monetary and fiscal policy are parts of a single process, not alternatives. In the early stages, money may have to be created to finance the deficit; the spending of this money generates the extra saving needed to "pay for" the investment; the rise in national income improves public revenues, thus helping the deficit to fall.

Contrary to a widespread view, the deficit does not impose a burden on future generations. There is no repayment burden because the government, unlike private individuals, can and normally does repay its maturing debts by borrowing again. (In the last resort, it can print money).

As for the interest burden that is said to arise when the interest is paid by taxation rather than by fresh borrowing, it is merely a transfer payment. Income is transferred from taxpayers to bond-holders. In the case of the UK, most of these bond-holders are domestic. The transfer is therefore a redistribution rather than a loss of income.

If, however, the public deficit is cut now, there will undoubtedly be a burden on both present and future generations. Income and profits will be lowered straight away; profits will fall, pension funds will be diminished, investment projects cancelled or postponed, schools not rebuilt – with the result that future generations will be worse off, having been deprived of assets they might otherwise have had.

The Keynesian theory contradicts the Osborne-Trichet doctrine that private spending is depressed because of fears about the sustainability or future cost of the deficit. The correct causal explanation is that private spending is depressed because total demand in the economy is depressed. The deficit is the consequence, not the cause, of depressed business expectations. It is "nature's way" of sustaining economic activity in the face of a collapse of business confidence.

Nevertheless, confidence is a psychological phenomenon. Irrational though the fear of a recession-induced deficit may be, it is a fact that governments have to face. So they should aim to maintain total spending in a way that reinforces rather than diminishes business confidence.

One way would be to cut taxes by the same amount as they cut their own spending. This would imply a reduction of taxes by about £100bn over five years. This might appeal to the right, as over a period of years it would reduce the size of the state. But the effect of tax-cutting on economic activity is uncertain. A better way would be to offset any market-appeasing cuts in current spending by an increase in capital spending. A recession is an ideal time to "bring the country up to date", since labour and capital will both be cheaper than in boom times.

The £38bn high-speed rail link from London to Birmingham and beyond, unveiled in March by Lord Adonis, the former transport secretary, is a perfect example. Like the smaller rail electrification schemes, it is not "shovel ready", but a determined government could get it going long before the planned start in 2017. It would set up an immediate demand on the construction industries while also offering returns in the long run.

Former chancellor Alistair Darling's scheme for a Green Investment Bank to invest in renewable energy and energy efficiency is another example. Industry experts predict that up to £37.5bn will be needed each year to upgrade or replace our old power plants over the next decade. Mr Darling's £2bn plan was a step in the right direction – a step that was then retracted in Mr Osborne's Budget.

A government whose animating spirit was Lloyd George rather than George Osborne would ask the public to subscribe to a National Recovery Loan of £100bn, to be spent over five years, to equip the UK with a modern transport system, energy-efficient housing and new power plants, and up-to-date schools. Austerity in the capital budget is the worst possible remedy for a slump.

Michael Kennedy is a former economic adviser to the Treasury.

11. Fixing the Right Hole
Project Syndicate | August 17, 2010

All economies recover in the end. The question is how fast and how far. When Keynes talked of persisting 'under-employment' he did not mean that, following a big shock, economies stay frozen at one unchanging level of under-activity. But he did think that, without an external stimulus, recovery from the lowest point would be slow, uncertain, weak, and liable to relapse. In short, his 'under-employment equilibrium' is a gravitational pull rather than a fixed condition. This is a situation which Alan Greenspan has aptly described as a 'quasi-recession', a better phrase than 'double-dip recession'. It is a situation of anaemic recovery, with bursts of excitement punctuated by collapses. It is the situation we are in today.

Contrary to Keynes, orthodox economics believes that, after a big shock, economies will 'naturally' return to their previous trend rate of growth, provided that governments balance their budgets and stop stealing resources from the private sector. The theory underlying it has been explained in the July Bulletin of the European Central Bank. Debt-financed public spending will 'crowd out' private spending either if it causes a rise in real interest rates or if it leads households to increase their saving because they expect to pay higher taxes later. In these cases a fiscal stimulus will not only have no effect; the economy will be worse off because public spending is inherently less efficient than private spending.

The Bulletin's authors do not believe that such complete 'crowding out' actually happened in the last two years. They explain why. If there are unemployed resources, extra government spending can 'crowd in' on private spending by creating additional demand in the economy which would otherwise not be there. Summarizing the evidence, the Bulletin finds that fiscal stimuli in the Eurozone have caused Eurozone GDP to be 1.3 per cent higher over the period 2009-2010 than it would otherwise have been.

The evidence of a positive effect is even stronger for the United States. In a recent paper, economists Alan Blinder and Mark Zandl find that the total stimulus policy adopted in 2009-2010 (including TARP) averted another Great Depression. Fiscal expansion alone (to make the direct comparison with the ECB Bulletin) caused US GDP to be 3.4 per cent higher over 2009-2010 than it would otherwise have been.

However the cutters have a fall-back position. The problem with fiscal stimuli, they say, is that they destroy confidence in the finances of the governments undertaking them, and this lack of confidence impedes recovery. So a credible deficit reduction programme is now needed to 'consolidate' recovery'.

What is it about cutting the deficit which is supposed to 'restore confidence'? Well, it 'may' lead consumers to believe that a permanent tax reduction will also take place in the near future. This will have a positive wealth effect and increase private consumption. (This is known as the expansionary fiscal contraction hypothesis.) But why on earth should consumers believe that cutting a deficit, and raising taxes now, will lead to tax cuts later on?

Well, fiscal consolidation, the Bulletin says, 'might' lead investors to expect an improvement in the supply-side of the economy. But it is unemployment, loss of skills and human self-confidence, and investment cancellations that hit the supply side.

Or 'credible announcement and implementation' of a fiscal consolidation strategy 'may' diminish the risk premium associated with government debt issuance. This will reduce real interest rates and make the 'crowding-in' of private spending more likely. But real interest rates on long-term government debt in the USA, Japan, Germany, and the UK are already close to zero. Not only do investors view the risks of depression and deflation as greater than those of default, but bonds are being preferred to equities for the same reason. Finally, the reduction of government borrowing requirements 'might' benefit output in the long-run from lower long-term interest rates. Of course, low long term interest rates are necessary for recovery. But so are profit expectations, and these depend on buoyant demand. However cheap it is for businessmen to borrow, they will not do so if they see no demand for their products.

These Bulletin arguments look to me like scraping the bottom of the intellectual barrel. The truth is that it's not the fear of government bankruptcy but governments' determination to balance their books which lowers business confidence, by reducing expectations of employment, incomes, and orders. It's not the hole in the budget but the hole in the economy which is the problem.

Let us assume, though, that the ECB is right and that fears of 'unsound finance' are holding back the recovery of the economy. The question still needs to be asked: are such fears rational? Are they not grossly exaggerated in the existing circumstances (except, possibly, in countries like Greece)? If so, is it not the duty of official bodies like the European Central Bank to challenge irrational beliefs about the economy rather than pander to them?

The trouble is that the present crisis finds governments intellectually disabled, because their theory of the economy is in a mess. Events and common sense drove them to deficit finance in 2009-2010, but they have not abandoned the theory which tells them that that depressions cannot happen, and that deficits are therefore always harmful (except in war!). So now they vie with each other in their haste to cut off the life-line which they themselves created. Policy-makers need to re-learn their Keynes, explain him clearly, and apply him, not invent pseudo-rational arguments for prolonging the recession.

12. The Failure of Labour
Northern Ireland Economic Conference, Belfast | September 29, 2010

I.

How much do people mind the deficit? Do they lie awake at night worrying about it? Do they have nightmares about it?

I tended to dismiss such thoughts as fanciful. Households and businesses, I thought, naturally worried about their own budgets, but not about the government's budget.

I therefore tended to assume that the government had enough freedom over its own budget to do what it thought best for the country, without coming under undue popular pressure to 'balance its books'.

Of course there were the 'markets'. But it didn't seem to me the markets were putting pressure on our government to 'balance the books'. After all they have been lending to Treasury long-term at 3 per cent. This is historically very low. It does not suggest any great fear of default or inflation. The markets can certainly make their displeasure felt, as Greece, Portugal, Ireland, and Spain have discovered. But it did not seem to me that a British government, of whatever stripe, faced this particular problem.

But I was brought up short by Alastair Darling in his speech of 27th September at the Labour party conference. The Evening Standard's headline was: 'Failure to cut debt would be electoral disaster, says Darling'. He is reported as saying:

> 'Whatever our message, it's got to strike a chord with millions of ordinary people as being realistic and credible. People know there is a deficit. They know it needs to come down. If we deny that, frankly people will not listen to you'.

So, it seems, people do worry about the deficit, perhaps even have nightmares about it. The Coalition, Darling implied, has struck the right chord.

Darling comes across as a solid citizen, in tune with ordinary people. So I ask myself: what is it that ordinary people fear or dislike about the deficit? I have come up with two answers.

First, people think of the government's finances very much as they think of their own household's finances.

Every household knows that it has to balance its books. If it is spending more than it's earning, it either has to earn more or spend less. Spending less means saving more. Yes it can borrow, but borrowing is for emergencies, and has to be repaid. It is better to stay out of debt. True enough, households went on a huge debt-financed spending spree. Now is the day of reckoning: the wages of sin have to be paid. Households also know that a lot of their spending is 'wasteful' – things they can do without. And they assume the same is true of governments.

Ordinary people, I suspect, think of the government as a huge household, which is currently spending much more than it is earning. So it has to increase its earnings – raise taxes – or reduce its spending, or some mixture of both, and set aside money for repaying its debt, just like the millions of smaller households in the land.

I believe that an analogy like this underlines much of the popular feeling that it's time for the government to start balancing its books.

But the analogy is not, perhaps, enough to create the demand. People also think of the impact of the national debt on their own finances. When they think of the government 'paying back' the national debt, they understand that it is they – the taxpaying citizens – who will be doing the paying. So they want to stop the growth of the National Debt, and that means reducing the deficit as quickly as possible. It's the debt not the deficit which looms largest in people's minds. Unless the books are balanced quickly, the burden on present and future tax payers will skyrocket. In fact it already portends a new age of austerity.

So the demand for retrenchment comes both from the analogy between households and governments and from the implied financial link between the two.

These are instinctual responses. But they are inflamed by politicians. David Cameron has said that 'the government deficit is just like credit card debt'. George Osborne has repeatedly pointed out that government borrowing is simply postponed taxation.

However, these are not the only instinctual responses. There is also, I would say, a strong instinctual understanding that cutting the deficit is likely to cost jobs. This is the trade union position. It was the great fault of the Labour Party leadership that it failed to develop a persuasive narrative capable of giving this instinct voice.

One should not underestimate the effect of language. Politicians use language to create a particular kind of narrative. The phrase 'deficit denial' is a conscious echo of the phrase 'Holocaust denial'. Another is the appropriation by the cutters of the word 'confidence'. Only a 'credible' programme of deficit reduction, it is claimed, will restore the 'confidence' of the markets in the government's solvency. Indeed the Coalition argues that it is only the announcement of the austerity package in June which has kept borrowing so cheap and allowed the British government to retain its AAA rating. This claim is made despite the fact that the Labour government was able to borrow just as cheaply.

An alternative narrative was readily available but was not used. A Keynesian would say that the enlargement of the deficit is the natural result of the collapse of private spending. It was only the government's willingness to allow public deficits to grow as the economy shrank that prevented another Great Depression. If, before recovery is secure, the government cuts its own spending, everyone in the economy will have less to spend, and there will be a further decline in aggregate demand, which will prolong or even deepen the recession. There will be no 'crowding in' of private spending if aggregate demand is too low. A Keynesian would certainly recognise the importance of 'confidence'. But he would say that the most important ingredient of business confidence is a full order book.

The reason the Labour leadership could not use this alternative narrative is that it was committed to a deficit reduction programme almost as drastic as that introduced by the Coalition. A cogent Keynesian stance would have been to avoid any commitments to cutting, and simply say the deficit would be managed in the light of economic circumstances. Intellectual room should have been left for a further fiscal stimulus if the recovery showed signs of stalling.

By not taking a principled stand of this kind, the last government lost the rhetorical battle. It couldn't openly say 'without a large deficit there will be no proper recovery'. It left the running to those who simply said that 'you can't spend money you haven't got'. It couldn't say 'the rise in the deficit and national debt is mainly a consequence of the shrinking of the economy: more borrowing for recovery now will mean less borrowing later'. Here are some interesting figures. In 1919 the National Debt stood at 135 per cent of GDP – as a result of heavy wartime borrowing. By 1920, after a year's inflationary boom it was down to 130 per cent. By 1922 it was up to 171 per cent? Why? Because there had been a huge deflation and rise in unemployment in 1921. In the deflationary decade of the 1920s, the debt hardly reduced at all. Nothing could more clearly illustrate the fact that the debt falls when the economy rises and rises when the economy falls.

There are other points Labour could have made. Unlike households, governments don't have to repay their debt. They can borrow almost without limit, especially from their own people. If interest rates go up, they can print more money to force them down again. Printing money won't cause inflation to go up if there is a lot of unused capacity. Another myth Labour could have attacked is the one which says the national debt is 'a burden on future generations'. Provided the debt is mainly held by British citizens, there is no net loss of income to future generations from any debt repayment: it is a matter of future taxpayers repaying future bondholders.

II.

In practice, most expert opinion expects that cutting the deficit will reduce Britain's growth rate in the short and medium term. But they say this is the price we will have to pay for longer-term benefits. Some of them try to manipulate expectations downwards by talking of a 'new normal' of tepid growth. In this view, the boom was the illusion, the slump the return of reality.

The experts offer one escape route from the deflationary effects of the cuts: printing money, or quantitative easing. This is supposed to have two effects, both supportive of recovery. Both come about through forcing down interest rates. The drop in Treasury yields will lower borrowing costs for householders and businesses, helping to stimulate consumption, business investment and housing. It will also cause the exchange rate to depreciate, helping exports. But both effects are highly uncertain.

Here is some evidence from the United States:

The Fed purchased $1.25 trillion in mortgage assets last year. Figures show it didn't go into bank lending. As it turns out, it went back onto the balance sheet of the Federal Reserve, i.e. banks simply paid back the Fed by buying back short-dated securities. There is similar evidence from UK, hence increasingly desperate calls from our politicians for banks to 'start lending'.

How much of an impact would $2 trillion in QE2 give the US economy? Not much, according to former Fed governor Larry Meyer. Meyer estimates that a $2 trillion asset purchase program would: 1) lower Treasury yields by 50bp; 2) increase GDP growth by 0.3 per cent in 2011 and 0.4 per cent in 2012; and 3) lower the unemployment rate by 0.3 per cent by the end of 2011 and 0.5 per cent by the end of 2012. However, Meyer admits that these may be 'high-end estimates'. That is not much bang for the buck.[6]

If banks are not lending now, with what seems like lots of reserves, then what is to make us think that another couple trillion dollars or billion pounds in QE will make them feel like they have too much money in their vaults?

If it is because they don't have enough capital, then adding liquidity to the system will not help that. If it is because they don't feel they have creditworthy customers, do we really want banks to lower their standards? Isn't that what got us into trouble last time? If it is because businesses don't want to borrow all that much because of the

---

6 I am indebted to investment analyst John Maudlin's weekly newsletter, Thoughts from the Frontline.

uncertain times, will easy money make that any better? As someone said, "I don't need more credit, I just need more customers." Keynes made the same point in the 1930s: it is not the printing of the money, but the spending of the money which stimulates the economy.

But what about the other escape route: exchange rate devaluation? Sterling has fallen by 20 per cent against the dollar and Euro since the beginning of the crisis, but the UK's current account deficit has widened to £8bn. Currency depreciation is good for exports if one has something to export.

Here we come face to face with one of the great fantasies of the Thatcher revolution, fully shared by New Labour: viz. that the service economy can provide a complete replacement for manufacturing industry. The main cause of our growing current account imbalance is our growing trade deficit in manufactured goods. On past trends the trade deficit will continue to grow. This will cause the pound to fall further.

But as Dr. Alan Reece, chairman of Pearson Engineering wrote in 2007:

'the UK will no longer have the ability to increase significantly the output of exports: there are no longer the factories or skilled workers and scientists and engineers required for this. There is no sign of any reduction in the rate at which manufacturing is being moved overseas....This is the main reason for the disappearance of manufacturers of power stations, ships and ship repairs, motor cars, trucks, tractors and other farm machinery, medical scanners etc.[7]

Manufacturing has once more borne the brunt of the recent collapse in output, and despite some recovery is still 10 per cent down on pre-recession levels.

III.

My conclusion is that we can't rely on QE2 or exchange rate depreciation to counter the effects of deficit reduction on aggregate demand. Labour can no longer refuse to commit itself to a definite programme of deficit reduction, because it already had one under Darling. What it can do is to switch the emphasis from deficit reduction to capital spending. In other words, we should revive the distinction, however fuzzy it has become, between current and capital spending. We should aim to balance the 'normal' budget, but grow the capital budget. We would then come

7 APR Newsletter January 2007

out of the recession with new assets. A time of unemployed resources is the ideal time for accelerated investment in schools, universities, hospitals, houses, transport infrastructure, and green technology. A programme like this will not only lift the economy out of recession; but it will create a demand on the manufacturing sector which will better secure our long term growth than reliance on financial and 'creative' services and outsourcing. This is a programme which will more easily commend itself to the public than what it believes is purely wasteful spending on current consumption. It combines intellectual cogency with at least the chance of popular appeal. It provides an opportunity to show what the government can and should do.

13. Britain's Austerity Apostles Duck the Debate
Financial Times | October 13, 2010

Next week the parliamentary battle over cuts will start up again. The chancellor, George Osborne, will say the government's programme of fiscal retrenchment is necessary to "restore confidence". Alan Johnson, his shadow, will say it threatens the "fragile recovery". The government plans to cut public spending by 10 per cent over four years as part of its deficit reduction plan. This will extract 5 per cent out of a shrunken economy. It is the most audacious axe-cutting exercise in almost a century, double the size of the cuts in the 1930s, equalled only by the 1921 Geddes Axe, which cut government spending by 11 per cent in two years. Labour says it is too much, too fast.

The two positions are clear enough, the arguments underlying them less so. What macroeconomic theory do the budget hawks have to subscribe to, to believe that taking £100bn out of the economy in the next four years will produce recovery? And what do the budget doves need to believe to claim the cutters are wrong?

David Cameron, Mr Osborne, and Nick Clegg appear to believe in something called "crowding out". This is the view that for every extra pound the government spends, the private sector spends one pound less. Jobs created by stimulus spending are jobs lost by the decline of private spending. Any stimulus to revive the economy is doubly damned: not only does it fail to stimulate, but, because government spending is less efficient than private, it reduces the economy's longer term recovery potential.

Applied to the deficit, the "crowding out" thesis takes two forms. The first is "Ricardian equivalence". Government borrowing is simply deferred taxation, because it produces no revenue to pay for it. Households save more to pay the higher taxes they expect. This means that any extra income created by the deficit will be saved, not spent. Net stimulus: zero.

The other leg of the "crowding out" argument is that government borrowing causes interest rates to rise. There is a fixed lump of saving. The more the government borrows, the more private borrowers will have to pay for their loans.

A refinement of this argument is "psychological crowding out". In this version it is not a shortage of saving, but a shortage of confidence in the government's creditworthiness – due to a fear of default – which causes interest rates to rise. Either way the deficit "crowds out" private investment. Net stimulus: zero.

The supposed implication of this type of argument is that in the short-run the deficit can do no good; and that in the slightly longer term it harms the potential for recovery. What the cutters have to believe is that every pound of deficit reduction will be matched by an extra pound of private sector spending. That is, if the government weren't spending this money, the private sector would be, and making much better use of it. Mr Osborne's programme is a beautiful cure for recession, provided there's no recession to cure!

Keynesians do not deny the possibility of "psychological crowding out": markets are subject to all kinds of irrational hopes and fears. But what the cutters mean by "crowding out" can normally only happen at full employment. At full employment, extra public spending obviously subtracts from private spending. But this is not the position we are in today.

What Keynesians say is that when resources are unemployed, government borrowing is not deferred taxation: it brings resources into use that would otherwise be idle, and thus increases the government's revenues without having to raise taxes. When the government borrows money for which there is no current business use, this increases people's incomes and therefore the saving needed to finance the borrowing, without interest rates having to rise. And though confidence problems may occur even in an under-employed economy, the probability of the UK government defaulting on its debt is, if not zero, extremely low.

In short, the "crowding out" argument is false. The problem is not the expansion of the deficit but the shrinkage of the economy. The deficit is the stimulant the economy needs to start growing again: its withdrawal guarantees stagnation or worse.

Why aren't we having this argument? The reason is that, against its instincts, the last Labour government accepted the pre-Keynesian economics of the cutters and sought only to ease the pain of the axe. To promise to cut a little less, and a little slower, than the coalition is an improvement, but not an alternative economic strategy. Only Ed Balls has the economic confidence and pugnacity to argue the Keynesian case. For political reasons he has been denied the shadow chancellor's job.

I would sum up this way. When an economy is growing to trend with a low level of unemployment, "crowding out" applies, and the budget ought to be balanced at modest level of taxes and spending. But when it has large unemployed resources, the Keynesian theory is best, and the government should not be ashamed of running a deficit. A properly Keynesian opposition would say that the budget balance should be dictated by economic circumstances, not by some arbitrary timetable: who knows what the situation will be in two, three, four years' time? But I doubt if this opposition will have the courage to do so.

14a. When confidence is shattered
New Statesman | October 25, 2010

I.

In economics, you cannot convict your opponents of error, but only convince them. Economics isn't like physics; you can't conduct controlled experiments to prove or disprove your theories. History provides a very partial way of overcoming this weakness. No events repeat themselves exactly, but past events offer some kind of test of current theories about the economy. The main question of current interest is the effect of fiscal consolidation.

The programme of fiscal consolidation has just been unveiled by George Osborne. The claim behind it is that slashing the deficit – removing £123bn from the economy over the next five years, partly by raising taxes, mostly by cutting spending – will make the economy recover faster and more vigorously from the recession. This theory goes under the name of "expansionary fiscal contraction".

It became popular in the 1980s as a counter to Keynesian orthodoxy at a time when fiscal policy was in flux. President Ronald Reagan, while proclaiming strict fiscal rectitude, in fact ran unprecedented (for that era) peacetime budget deficits. For Keynesians the US boom of the 1980s was the direct consequence of the huge dollops of extra demand being pumped into the American economy, mainly for military spending. Keynesian economists warned against premature curtailment of this stimulus. As Ralph Bryant, John Helliwell and Peter Hooper[8] put it "an unanticipated cut in US federal purchases could have a substantial negative on the level of US real output for several years". But two other economists, Gerhard Fels and Hans-Peter Frölich[9], studied a different episode, that of fiscal consolidation in the Federal Republic of Germany. They noted that the "anti-Keynesian" policy there had coincided with a rapid recovery of the economy from the 1981-2 recession, and attributed this "coincidence" largely to the favourable effect of consolidation on expectations in the private sector. A similar conclusion was drawn from Geoffrey Howe's 1981 Budget. Indeed, it became part of Thatcherite folklore that Howe's fiscal retrenchment was shortly followed by a resumption of rapid growth, despite the dire warnings by hundreds of Keynesian economists.

The proposition that cuts in government spending can grow the economy relies on "Ricardian equivalence" – the oft-repeated claim,

---

8   Bryant et al. Macroeconomic Policies in an Interdependent World, 1989
9   Economic Policy 4 (April 1987)

made by the likes of Osborne, that government borrowing is just deferred taxation. If households and investors factor in future levels of taxation when they're making spending decisions now, a stimulus would have no effect on economic growth. Households will simply cut back on their consumption in anticipation of inevitable tax increases. So public spending "crowds out" private spending.

But now let's ask: what would households and firms do in response to a cut in government spending? Ricardian equivalence says that reduced borrowing will create an expectation of lower taxes in the future (even if in the short term the deficit reduction includes tax rises). Freed of the burden of future taxes, private agents will happily spend more now, providing the required boost to demand when the government steps back. Increased demand means more jobs created in the private sector. The resulting increase in spending may well be enough to outweigh the money taken out of the economy by the government, and thus increase output overall.

The effect on investor and consumer confidence is likely to be even greater if spending cuts are seen to prevent an even more painful readjustment in the future. This can happen if the national debt is seen to reach an extreme level. Dispelling the fear of a Greece-style debt crisis might contribute more to growth than the loss of public money propping it up.

The other way cutting the deficit can reverse "crowding out" is by leading to lower interest rates. According to this argument, government borrowing drives up interest rates, because at a fixed level of saving the government demand for borrowing increases the price private borrowers will pay for access to finance. As a result, government spending "crowds out" private spending, substituting on a one-to-one basis. So if government borrowing falls, interest rates will fall allowing private firms to borrow more cheaply.

Thus, a reduction in the deficit today might be good for the economy tomorrow under three conditions: if is taken to signal lower taxes; if it leads to lower interest rates; and if it reduces the risk of "bad news" such as default, inflation, and so on – that is, if it leads to greater confidence.

What does the historical record tell us? The OECD claims that in the past thirty years, around half of the fiscal contractions in the EU have been followed by an acceleration in growth. There is no shortage of historical episodes offered as models for today's cuts – Canada, Ireland, Denmark – but here three examples from British economic history seem most relevant.

II.

The last time public spending was cut on the scale proposed by Osborne was in 1921-22, with the "Geddes Axe", carried out under a previous Conservative-Liberal coalition government.

During the First World War, government spending, taxes and state involvement in the economy had expanded enormously. The war effort had been financed through borrowing, and the result was a sharp increase in government debt, which peaked in 1919 at 135 per cent of GDP – compare the projected peak of 70 per cent in 2013. The wartime scale of deficit spending brought with it an inflationary boom immediately after the war, while demobilisation and the sell-off of military assets brought fiscal surpluses. But there was a quickening current of middle-class discontent at the burden of taxation, which manifested itself in the "anti-waste" movement.

The Anti-Waste League, founded by 1st Viscount Rothermere, owner of the *Daily Mail*, campaigned against what was seen as wasteful government expenditure, winning three "safe" Conservative seats in by-elections in the first half of 1921. In the end, the political pressure on the government proved too great. David Lloyd George renounced his promises of "homes fit for heroes" and an independent committee of businessmen, led by Sir Eric Geddes, was asked to produce savings of £100m in addition to the £75m the Treasury had already extracted from the departments. By cutting expenditure, the government argued, it would make room for tax cuts, and find money to pay down the debt.

In the end, Geddes proposed £87m of extra cuts, and while departments did not quite reach the Geddes Axe target, central government current spending fell by about £100bn in today's value over five years – not entirely unlike today's projected cuts. Although the majority of the savings were made in defence, the short-sighted focus on reducing waste damaged areas vital for long-term economic growth, notably secondary education for poorer children. The cuts in the Budget hit an economy already suffering from a huge fall in output. Monetary policy was not eased to offset fiscal contraction, because interest rates were kept high to help the pound regain its pre-war parity with the dollar: a tactical blunder that earned the wrath of John Maynard Keynes.

The result was eight years of anaemic growth, punctuated by the General Strike of 1926, with unemployment of insured workers never falling below 10 per cent. This situation was the origins of Keynes's later concept of "under-employment equilibrium". There is a further lesson for today. The shrinkage of the economy in 1921 and 1922 caused the national debt to grow from 135 per cent of GDP in 1919 to 180 per cent in 1923, and though it subsequently came down it was higher in 1929 than it had been at the end of the war.

Move forward to the Great Depression. The Wall Street crash of 1929 brought a global collapse in demand. By 1931 UK unemployment had almost reached 20 per cent. Concerns about the solvency of the Labour government's finances led the Chancellor, Philip Snowden, to set up an independent committee under Sir George May, formerly of the Prudential, to recommend cuts in public expenditure. Projecting a deficit of £120m for 1932-3, the committee demanded £96m of cuts, mostly to come from benefits and wages, and £24m of extra taxes. The hole in the government's budget was 10 per cent of public spending, about the same as today's, though it was to be closed in one year rather than five.

It needed a National Government, formed by the Labour Prime Minister, Ramsay MacDonald, with the support of the Conservative and Liberal parties but against the opposition of his own, to deliver the cuts demanded by the May Committee. But these failed to restore confidence, and Britain was forced off the gold standard a month after their enactment in September 1931, following a "mutiny" at Invergordon of naval ratings facing pay cuts. Keynes wrote in the *New Statesman* at the time that the May Committee cuts would add some 400,000 to the unemployed, diminishing tax receipts and reducing the "saving" on the budget to just £50m. "At the present time all governments have large deficits," he wrote. "They are nature's remedy for preventing business losses from being…so great as to bring production altogether to a standstill."

One can point to four years of solid growth from 1933-1937, but it is hard to argue that this had anything to do with an "expansionary fiscal contraction". Rather it was Britain's abandonment of the gold standard that was the decisive event. This had two expansionary effects: interest rates could come down to 2 per cent, where they stayed for the rest of the 1930s, and the pound lost 30 per cent of its value. This first enabled the Treasury to convert the national debt to lower interest rates, and sparked off a private housing boom; the second boosted exports for a year and a half until the United States devalued the dollar, too. The decline in GDP during the Depression years caused the national debt to rise from 160 per cent in 1929 to 180 per cent in 1933, higher than during the war. Despite the recovery, interrupted by a "double dip" in 1937, unemployment never fell below 12 per cent for the rest of the decade.

Osborne's think-tank acolytes often invoke the spirit of Geoffrey Howe's 1981 Budget. His savage programme of cuts – designed primarily to help bring down inflation – took £4bn, or 2 per cent, out of the economy when unemployment was already rising. Howe's plan ran up against the Keynesian orthodoxy of the day. In March 1981, 364 economists, including the current governor of the Bank of England, Mervyn King, wrote an open letter to the *Times*, predicting that government policy would "deepen the depression, erode the industrial base of our economy and threaten its social and political stability". Almost before the ink was dry on the letter, the economy emerged from recession, growing by 3.3 per cent on average over the following five years. (Inflation also fell from 17.8 per cent in 1980 to 4.3 per cent in 1982). A textbook example of an expansionary fiscal contraction?

Not quite. In a retrospective report on the merits of the 1981 budget, published by the Institute of Economic Affairs[10], none of the contributors believes it was the Budget cuts themselves which produced recovery. Rather, it was the monetary loosening which accompanied them: interest rates were cut by 2 per cent and restrictions eased on bank lending. Tim Congdon, the most skilful defender of Howe's budget strategy, argues: "the [presumably adverse] macroeconomic effects of the £4bn tax increase in the 1981 Budget were smothered by the much larger and more powerful effects of changes in monetary policy'.

Stephen Nickell, formerly of the Monetary Policy Committee, and an unrepentant signatory of the letter, agrees. He does point out, however, that as unemployment continued rising and did not start falling for five years, the fiscal contraction widened the output gap and the economy failed to grow to trend. So the defence of the Howe Budget rests on the assertion that budget cuts were needed to bring down long-term interest rates, with private spending being "crowded in" by the contraction of government spending. With large numbers of people unemployed, this is not very plausible.

Where cheaper money may have had a favourable impact was on asset prices. It was the boom in house prices and financial assets which led the Thatcher recovery. Today, Osborne apparently puts his faith in monetary loosening to offset the effects of his fiscal consolidation.

III.

Some conclusions can be drawn from these episodes. First, the fiscal contraction was never followed by economic growth strong enough to replace the output lost in the preceding slump. In all three cases it is likely that it made the slump worse than it would have been. Second, and because of the last factor, it failed to reduce the national debt. The national debt as a share of GDP rises in periods of stagnation and falls

10   *Were 364 Economists All Wrong?* (2006)

in when times are prosperous. Third, in all cases it led to considerable social and political unrest: we have only to think of the 1926 General Strike, the hunger marches in the 1930s, and the miners' strike of 1984-5.

Two of the three episodes considered – those of 1931 and of 1981-2 – were followed shortly by economic revival. However, a correlation is not a cause. By general consent it was cheap money, and not fiscal contraction, which brought about the recovery, and the deficit hawks have failed to establish that it was the fiscal consolidation which caused the cheap money. Indeed, on *a priori* grounds this is highly unlikely. To the extent that Budget retrenchment reduces the national income to less than what it would have been, it reduces saving and money supply, and thus leads to interest rates higher than they would otherwise have been.

So we are brought back to the question of confidence. One can imagine a set of circumstances in which fiscal consolidation will have a sufficiently invigorating effect to cause a recovery. I would suggest, however, that this can only happen in the context of extreme events. If a government is felt to have lost all control, if the size of the debt is so vast that it threatens imminent default, then a decisive change of policy can have a decisive effect. Britain was hardly in this position last April, despite all the efforts of Conservative spokesmen to play up the imminence of the danger facing the country under Labour rule.

This illustrates the point that one cannot, and should not, reduce all economic policy to matters of psychology. It leads to the view that fatuous expressions of confidence, provided they are repeated often enough, can overcome the effects of disturbing events. For this to be true, one has to assume a great deal of irrationality in the electorate. Some irrationality there surely is, but it is more reasonable to believe that if a businessman faces a declining demand for his products he will curtail his production, rather than expand it.

So, what are the prospects for Osborne's cuts? They will directly worsen immediate growth prospects, as the Office of Budget Responsibility concedes, and they will not in themselves bring about offsetting reductions in long-term interest rates. For this, we need quantitative easing (printing money) and it is no secret that this is what the Chancellor relies on to vindicate his policy. Yet one would be wrong to think this is a cure-all. For one thing, it never brought about complete recovery in the past. Second, its main influence is on asset prices. Housing and construction benefit especially from low interest rates, but do we want to stimulate another housing boom fuelled by cheap credit? Moreover, most of an economy's investment is more sensitive to the level of demand than to the cost of capital, so that even large reductions in interest rates might have quite a small effect on activity.

Quantitative easing is Osborne's last throw. But the injection of £200bn of new money in 2009 failed to revive lending and borrowing on the scale needed for robust recovery, and it is not clear why the Chancellor and the governor of the Bank of England expect another monetary injection to do any better now. Demand is expected to fall further and new unsecured lending is priced at 10.5 per cent despite a 0.5 per cent bank rate.

Keynes spelled out the alternatives we face today in 1932, in the thick of the Great Depression: "It may still be the case that the lender, with his confidence shattered by his experience, will continue to ask for new enterprise rates of interest which the borrower cannot expect to earn...If this proves to be the case there will be no means of escape from prolonged and perhaps interminable depression except by direct state intervention to promote and subsidise new investment." George Osborne be warned.

14b. Keynes would be on our side
Vince Cable
New Statesman I January 12, 2011

If anyone doubted it before, recent months have proved decisively that coalitions are quite consistent with radical policy change. What matters now for British politics is whether the coalition government's economic policies deliver a sustainable recovery.

The most controversial part of the debate relates to the speed at which the fiscal deficit should be corrected. It is not, however, a controversy within the coalition. The structural deficit is over 6 per cent of GDP - meaning that, even once the economy has recovered fully, the government would still be borrowing almost £100bn a year. In September 2009, I argued in a Reform pamphlet that, in balancing the risks of too rapid adjustment (threatening recovery) or delaying it (precipitating a deficit funding crisis), the next government should try to eliminate this deficit over five years. Now we are in government, that is exactly what we plan to do.

Despite all the controversy, the boundaries that define this debate are relatively narrow. The outgoing Labour government was already planning a fiscal tightening of 1.5 per cent of GDP in 2010/2011. The difference between its deficit reduction plan beyond 2010/2011 and that of the coalition amounts to roughly half a per cent of GDP per annum: well within the forecasting error. Such differences, though not trivial, hardly justify the titanic clash of economic ideas advertised in the commentaries or a threatened mobilisation of opposition comparable to the General Strike. For all the protesters shouting "No to cuts", this electoral term would always have been about public-sector austerity, no matter who won the election.

As in many economic policy disputes, much of the ideological rhetoric conceals different forecasting assumptions - in respect of the cyclical, as opposed to structural, deficit; the influence of asset prices on consumer behaviour; the impact of the unorthodox monetary policy of quantitative easing (QE) and its interaction with the velocity of circulation of money; and the weight to be attached to business confidence and sentiment in financial markets. Amid such uncertainty, economic policymaking is like driving a car with an opaque windscreen, a large rear-view mirror and poor brakes. To avoid the trap of self-justifying, competitive forecasting, the government has subcontracted its forecasts to an independent body, the Office for Budget Responsibility (OBR). As it happens, the OBR has produced the reassuring estimate that, on plausible assumptions, growth should improve, unemployment should fall and fiscal consolidation should ease to safe levels over the five-year life of this parliament. But even such an independent body can only point to a range of probabilities.

This lack of solid ground has failed to discourage serious people from invoking different economic philosophies to justify polarised positions. Increasingly, the debate is characterised in terms of John Maynard Keynes (in the "left" corner) v the reincarnations of his 1930s critics (in the "right" corner). Whatever their motivations, Nobel prizewinners and other economists are lining up with party politicians to re-enact the dramas of 80 years ago, like history buffs dressing up in armour to relive the battles of the English civil war.

This politicisation is odd, because Keynes was a liberal, not a socialist (nor even a social democrat). He showed no fundamental discomfort with the then modest levels of state spending in the economy, which amounted to half of today's level as a share of GDP. Keynes's policies were intended not to overthrow capitalism but to save it from a systemic malfunction - the problem of insufficient aggregate demand.

Despite the mischaracterisation of Keynes as a friend of socialism, the ongoing debates are valuable insofar as they illuminate vital bits of theory and evidence. In a recent *New Statesman* essay Robert Skidelsky provides a very good exposition of the Keynesian interpretation of current problems and solutions. I would like to continue the debate but argue that Keynes would be on my side, not his.

The main theoretical issue is what determines investment. As illustrated in the OBR's forecasts, growth is expected to come from a large increase in private-sector investment, after decades in which ever-increasing consumption has borne too much of the burden of fuelling growth. Keynes, too, was consistently preoccupied with how to sustain investment as the motor of economic growth and employment. The specific problem he grappled with was what happens during a slump, when intended saving seriously diverges from intended investment, such that there is a pool of excessive savings, which, in turn, depresses spending and the willingness of business to produce and employ workers.

The orthodox response was that interest rates would fall, increasing investment and reducing savings, thus restoring balance. Flexible wages would operate to restore full employment. Keynes showed that, sometimes, this equilibrating mechanism may not work without government intervention to support demand, particularly when deflationary conditions pertain. During periods of weak expected demand, consumers and businessmen hold back from spending and reinforce the deflationary trend. This is the mistake that governments of the interwar period perpetrated.

Few would now deny that Keynes's insight was correct, and it was put to good use in the co-ordinated global response to the financial crisis two years ago. This response reflected an understanding that, while Keynes's original analysis was based on a model of a closed economy, today's investment/savings imbalances manifest themselves at a global level (with the UK, like the US, importing savings). Nonetheless, modern Keynesians claim to hear the echo of a long-dead 1930s controversy in the coalition government's policy of seeking an investment-led recovery and at the same time reducing state-financed demand, through cutting the government's current spending and increasing tax receipts.

Skidelsky concludes his essay by quoting Keynes, writing on investment in 1932, in the depths of the Great Depression: "It may still be the case that the lender, with his confidence shattered by his experience, will continue to ask for new enterprise rates of interest which the borrower cannot expect to earn . . . There will be no means of escape from prolonged and, perhaps, interminable depression except by direct state intervention to promote and subsidise new investment."

In other words, there are times when only through government spending will the economy gain the growth in expected demand necessary to drag it out of a slump. The deflationary 1930s were certainly one such time. The question, however, is what relevance that insight has today.

Decision-making has to be evidence-based rather than dogmatic. At a macroeconomic level, there is now a wealth of experience of postwar fiscal adjustment in developed-market economies - more than 40 examples since the mid-1970s. This experience provides strong empirical support for the view that decisive rather than gradual budgetary adjustments, focusing on spending cuts, have been successful in correcting fiscal imbalances and have, in general, boosted rather than suppressed growth - the experience in Denmark in the 1980s, for example, as Francesco Giavazzi and Marco Pagano argued in 1990. A recent study by the International Monetary Fund determines that fiscal consolidation does, indeed, boost growth and employment but only in the long term (five years or more) and may have negative effects in the short run.

The overall conclusions are non-Keynesian. What explains this? One plausible explanation, from Olivier Blanchard of the IMF, is that the Keynesian model of fiscal policy works well enough in most conditions, but not when there is a fiscal crisis. In those circumstances, households and businesses react to increased deficits by saving more, because they expect spending cuts and tax increases in the future. At a time like this, fiscal multipliers decline and turn negative. Conversely, firm action to reduce deficits provides reassurance to spend and invest. Such arguments are sometimes described as "Ricardian equivalence"

- that deficits cannot stimulate demand because of expected future tax increases. While David Ricardo's name may have been misused to perpetuate an economic dogma - one popular in Germany - his mechanism could well explain behaviour in fiscal-crisis economies.

The Keynesian counteroffensive consists of several arguments. First, it is argued that "the myth of expansionary fiscal austerity" (Dean Baker, Centre for Economic Policy Research, October 2010) is based on extrapolating from the results of adjustment in boom conditions, or at least relatively favourable international conditions. As Keynes put it: "The boom, not the slump, is the right time for austerity at the Treasury."

Skidelsky rightly cites the "Geddes Axe" in 1921-22 and the Snowden cuts of 1931 as examples of badly timed austerity. However, Britain today cannot be said to be in a deflationary slump. There is annual growth of 2 to 2.5 per cent. Added to inflation of 3 to 3.5 per cent, the UK now has growth in the cash economy of over 6 per cent per annum - nothing like the conditions needed for a liquidity trap. Tradables, including the manufacturing sector, are growing in response to a 25 per cent devaluation and strong growth in Asia and parts of the EU. Private, non-financial companies are expected to achieve 10 per cent growth in capital spending in 2011/2012, based on CBI surveys. Unemployment is 7.9 per cent on the International Labour Organisation measure and 4.6 per cent on the claimant count, hardly comparable to the 20 per cent suffered in 1931. It is true that the economy is still recovering from the economic equivalent of a heart attack, which took place two years ago. But the intensive-care phase has passed. Current conditions in the economy are far closer to recovery than to slump, with manufacturing, in particular, enjoying robust growth and survey after survey of business leaders indicating that they are planning for expansion.

Second, Keynesian critics are overly dismissive of the importance of keeping down the cost of capital (by maintaining the confidence of lenders). Skidelsky wrote in his essay that "even large reductions in interest rates might have quite small effects on activity". Yet this was not Keynes's view at all. In his open letter to Franklin D Roosevelt in 1933, he argues: "I put in second place [after accelerated capital spending] the maintenance of cheap and abundant credit and, in particular, the reduction of long-term rates of interest . . . Such a policy might become effective in the course of a few months and I attach great importance to it."

The coalition has had demonstrable success in this area. As the perceived risks of a fiscal crisis have receded, ten-year-term government bond yields in the UK have fallen from 3.7 per cent in May to around 3.3 per cent and are now closer to those in Germany and France than those in the troubled southern periphery of the EU. To see what the alternative might have been, you need only look at other European countries where yields have risen by 2 per cent or more. Had this happened in Britain, with its eye-watering levels of private debt, the risk of a second dip into recession would have been very real.

A third and related point is that Skidelsky and others are inclined to dismiss arguments that rest on "matters of psychology" or "fatuous expressions of confidence". This is an odd criticism, as Keynes also relies heavily on the mass psychology of confidence induced by expansionary policies and on stimulating the "animal spirits" of entrepreneurs. It is especially odd in the wake of the global financial crisis, when loss of confidence in highly leveraged financial institutions caused widespread economic damage and at a point where highly leveraged governments are being subjected to the same degree of critical scrutiny.

One of the more worrying reactions of the Keynesian critics is their belief that Britain, in some undefined way, is immune from the kind of financial firestorm that occurred in the eurozone in April and May, or the repeated flare-ups from Greece through Spain and Portugal to Ireland since. Even some distinguished academic economists don't understand how volatile and vulnerable to speculative attack the capital markets have become. The cardinal error of the boom years was to assume that low, stable interest rates were a fact of life, when such conditions could vanish overnight. An important justification for our early action on the deficit was to remove any risk of a sterling debt crisis.

The fourth and final element of the Keynesian counteroffensive might be called the "plan B" problem: what if rapid cuts do have gravely depressive effects on economic activity and investment? Can a government, using fiscal discipline as a means of restoring confidence, produce an alternative plan?

There are several answers to this. The most important is that, while all sensible governments plan for contingencies, there is no reason to assume the need for a plan B or a plan C, because there is a credible plan A and every sign is that it is working.

Another observation is that tight fiscal policy can be expected to be offset by loose monetary policy. As Mervyn King said last June: "If prospects for growth were to weaken, the outlook for inflation would probably be lower and monetary policy could then respond." Indeed, our early recovery during the Depression is generally linked to leaving the gold standard in 1931 and enabling looser money. Though the effects of QE are not fully understood, it should be clear that it is effective - the fast growth of the cash economy since the easing began is evidence.

Furthermore, it is only through having a clear plan A that the government can claim to be well prepared if the economy takes an unexpected dip. As we have seen elsewhere in the world, the only countries that are capable of supporting their economies in a crisis are those that have the confidence of the bond market. Britain's credit is as good as it can be. Contrast this with our position going into the 2008-2009 recession: with a huge structural deficit and demonstrating no willingness to address it, the Labour government could afford very little stimulus (another point made both by me and by George Osborne in 2009).

It would be foolish to be complacent, however. I worry that the modern Keynesians are not bold enough and that the rather contrived indignation over the speed of deficit reduction distracts attention from more critical problems. We have, after all, just experienced the near collapse of the banking sector, the freezing of credit systems and the subsequent need to recapitalise banks leading to further credit restriction. The crisis was global but Britain's exceptional exposure to the global banks has left us disproportionately affected - if not quite as severely as Iceland or Ireland.

The economics of banking and credit crises was first explained properly by John Stuart Mill nearly 200 years ago. In modern times, the best analysis has come from Friedrich Hayek. As Meghnad Desai has put it: "The current crisis is very much a Hayekian crisis" - caused by excess credit, leading to bad investments that eventually collapsed. That is not to say Keynes was "wrong"; that would be as absurd as saying that Newton was "wrong" because he did not explain quantum phenomena. But we should be sceptical about Keynesian economists, however distinguished, who conspicuously failed to anticipate the financial crisis and now blithely ignore its consequences. Skidelsky's essay does not even make passing reference to the banking crisis, like someone dispensing advice on earthquake relief and reconstruction without any reference to past or future earthquakes.

We cannot ignore the causes of the crisis. That is why the government's deficit reduction programme, though necessary, is not sufficient. We still need to address the question of how to generate investment and sustainable growth. It will not happen automatically. Supply-side reforms will help: attracting inward investment; shifting taxation away from profitable, productive investment (as opposed to unproductive asset accumulation, as with property); reducing obstacles to productive activity; reforming corporate governance and takeover rules to encourage long-term - rather than speculative - investment; helping workers to adjust through training, retraining and a safety net of benefits.

But a central issue remains the high cost and low availability of capital in a low-interest environment. Real short-term interest rates are negative and real long-term rates close to zero. Capital is, in theory, cheap - and for those large companies that have access to capital markets or the confidence of the banks, borrowing has never been cheaper. But for smaller business borrowers that rely on the banking system, there is a continuing credit crunch, with high (often double-digit) interest rates, new charges or conditions, sometimes a blank refusal to offer any finance at all. Small companies are the backbone of our economy and, in their eagerness to deleverage, banks may squeeze the life out of productive enterprise. To remedy this problem requires an early move to counter the cyclical regulation of the banks and, in the wake of the Banking Commission, now sitting, structural reform of the banking sector.

The problem - of available capital failing to find its way into economic activity - goes wider than banking. Dieter Helm has described how there is huge, pent-up demand for infrastructure investment and abundant available savings, but the regulatory environment needs reform to reduce the cost of capital. There is what Keynes described as a problem of "liquidity preference", but it is not caused by lack of demand. Put simply, investors need reasonable reassurance that they will get their money back with decent, long-term rates of return and the ability to buy and sell their investment cheaply.

Keynes was right to argue that the state has a critical role to play in facilitating investment. Banking reform is one requirement, as is reform of the regulatory system to encourage private investment in public goods. Other innovations such as local tax increments and tolling can free up investment without undermining fiscal credibility. The government is already relaxing a little the deep cuts inherited from the Labour government in capital spending.

The serious debate for progressives should not centre on denying the need for discipline over public spending. If the British left follows Bob Crow and the National Union of Students to the promised land of the big spenders, it will enjoy short-term popularity at the expense of the coalition but it will also enter an intellectual and political blind alley. We need instead to reform the British state to create a banking system, incentives and institutions that will put safety first, not speculation, and will liberate new and sustainable investment. That is the challenge Keynes would have relished.

14c. Vince Cable is working. The coalition isn't.

Robert Skidelsky and David Blanchflower
New Statesman | January 24, 2011

Vince Cable's essay in the 17 January issue of the *New Statesman* ("Keynes would be on our side") is the first, and very welcome, sign of a senior coalition politician being willing to engage in a serious public debate on economic policy. Cable has written a well-argued – but ultimately unconvincing – defence of the coalition's economic strategy.

His first, and perhaps least interesting, argument is that the parties are in agreement about a deficit reduction policy: the only question is the speed of reduction. This may be so, but a consensus is not the same thing as the truth. Cable argues that it is appropriate to begin to pay off the deficit "over five years". It is important to point out, however, that there is no basis in economics for the imposition of a time period. This choice of five years is entirely arbitrary, as, indeed, was the time frame of the Labour government's less austere fiscal tightening plan.

The only sensible course was – and still is – to commit to reducing the deficit at a speed and by an amount determined by economic circumstances. This would have the benefit of allowing decision-makers to avoid taking a premature view on the size of the "structural deficit". Cable says it would have been 6 per cent of GDP even with "full recovery", but readers should know that there is considerable doubt about this number.

"Look after unemployment and the Budget will look after itself," was John Maynard Keynes's advice. This may not always be true but it is better than the coalition's current stance of: "Look after the Budget and unemployment will look after itself."

Paying off the deficit too quickly, on the basis of projections that even Cable concedes are highly uncertain, carries a far greater risk of a decade or more of lost output and social unrest and dislocation than a more measured path that is dependent on, for example, the economy hitting unemployment targets. When unemployment is far above any plausible "natural" rate, longer is likely to be better than shorter.

Cable seems to place a great deal of faith in the confidence-boosting effect of fiscal contractions. But the empirical evidence for this is far from convincing. An important study by Vincent Hogan[11] finds that the increase in private consumption produced by fiscal contraction is not sufficient to offset the direct effect of the reduction in public consumption.

---

11   Scandinavian Journal of Economics, 106(4), 2004

Another study, by Rita Canale and others, published by the University of Naples in 2007[12], concludes that fiscal contraction may be consistent with an expansion of aggregate demand if looser monetary policy concurrently leads to devaluation. But it is the monetary loosening, not the fiscal contraction, which has this effect.

In such cases it would be more accurate to say that economic recovery is possible despite fiscal consolidation. The question then is whether recovery might have been faster and more durable had fiscal and monetary policy both been expansionary. Cable argues that, had the coalition not acted decisively to reduce the deficit, Britain would have faced a "crisis of confidence" similar to that of Greece, which would have forced up the yield on government bonds. This is frequently asserted, but it is far-fetched. Even before the coalition's deficit reduction plan, the British government was able to borrow at historically low rates. Moreover, the US treasury bond rate is even lower than ours, without a deficit reduction plan. There are many reasons for these low bond yields, but one of them is surely the diminished appetite for risk, itself a product of economic stagnation.

In any case, Britain is not Greece. For one thing, Greece has spent more than half the years since independence, in 1829, in default; Britain has not defaulted once in that period.[13] In addition, the UK has its own central bank and a floating exchange rate, while Greece is stuck in monetary union.

Greece is characterised by endemic tax evasion, a poor tax collection infrastructure, parochial patronage policies, corruption and huge delays in the administrative courts dealing with tax disputes. This clearly does not resemble developments in the UK. Granted, there was always a risk that "contagion" would spread from Greece to Britain. But the Conservatives had planned to slash public spending before the Greek crisis flared up, as a matter of ideological conviction. Greece was the excuse, not the reason.

Cable then embarks on the project of enlisting Keynes on behalf of the coalition's policy. First, some clearing of the air: Keynes never denied that economies would recover from depressions without help from governments. What he argued was that countries would not regain full employment without an exogenous injection of demand. Without it, the business cycle would go on, but at a lower level of activity.

In short, without sufficient "stimulus", the employment and growth effects of a deep recession are long-lasting and likely to be large.

---

12   Rita Canale et al. "On Keynesian Effects of (Apparent) Non-Keynesian Policies, University of Naples Economics Discussion Paper No. 8, 2007
13   See Carmen M Reinhart and Kenneth S Rogoff, *This Time Is Different*, Princeton University Press, 2009, page 99

History bears this out. The UK and US did recover from the Great Depression, which reached its peak between 1929 and 1931, but the recovery was not strong enough to take them back to full employment for another eight years, when significant war spending started. Think, too, of the effects in the 1980s of the recession under Margaret Thatcher. UK unemployment was 5.3 per cent in May 1979 and remained above that level every month for the next 21 years until July 2000. There was another big collapse in output in 1937-38, as there was in 1987-89.

It is not enough to cite recoveries now in progress, or to chalk up growth rates, which recently have started to slow sharply. The question is whether current and projected growth rates will be strong and sustainable enough to restore full employment within some relatively short period, such as the life of this parliament. That seems unlikely.

Moreover, Cable severely underestimates the costs of prolonged underactivity. We need to take into account not just the output lost during the slump but the potential output lost in the subsequent periods of mediocre recovery. By 2015, the loss of output in the British economy from these two sources might well be in the order of 10 per cent. That is, the British economy might well be 10 per cent smaller than it would have been, had proper Keynesian policies been followed. This needs to be thought of in terms of the rusting away of human skills through persisting unemployment and failure to build the necessary infrastructure. As such, the knock-on effects go beyond 2015.

Cable is right to say that Keynes thought that the reduction of long-term interest rates had a vital role to play in sustaining any recovery. But he denied that it could happen naturally on its own, because, contrary to Cable's interpretation, he did not believe that there was a "pool of excess saving" in a slump. There are no "excessive savings" during a slump because the excess saving that caused the slump has been eliminated by the fall in income. That means there is no "natural" tendency for the interest rate to fall: the fall has to be brought about by central bank policy. This was the main goal of the Bank of England's recent £200bn quantitative easing (QE) policy.

More importantly, Keynes doubted whether the lowering of long-term interest rates would be enough to produce a full recovery. Again, the experience of the 1930s bears this out. "Cheap money" started a housing boom, which pulled the economy upwards, but it was never sufficient to restore full employment. The reason is that if profit expectations are sufficiently depressed, it might require negative real interest rates to produce a full-employment volume of investment. This is Keynes's liquidity trap.

Although we are not yet in this situation, bank lending remains limited despite QE, especially to small firms that are unable to issue bonds. Hence the velocity of circulation has not recovered to pre-crisis levels because the banks are limiting their lending so that they can rebuild their balance sheets and firms lack confidence to invest.

So, what are the prospects for strong recovery in the present policy regime? Cable notes, correctly, that the Office for Budget Responsibility has produced the reassuring estimate that, on plausible assumptions, there should be improving growth, falling unemployment and fiscal consolidation to safe levels over the five-year life of this parliament. This forecast is considerably more optimistic than the consensus and is probably subject to marked downside risks, both externally, from further unravelling of the sovereign debt crisis, and domestically, where demand looks weak.

The latest economic data shows a big increase in the size of the national debt and in the debt-to-GDP ratio. GDP growth is slowing, unemployment has started to rise again – youth unemployment is approaching a million once more – and real wages are falling. Job creation in the private sector in the most recent quarter was exactly nil, while the public sector culled 33,000 jobs. In our view, under present policies, unemployment is likely to rise over the life of this parliament.

Furthermore, business and consumer confidence has collapsed since May 2010. This is illustrated in the two charts [omitted]. The first shows Markit's purchasing managers' indices (PMIs) for manufacturing, services and construction. Despite the recent jump in the manufacturing PMI, the overall index for the month dropped sharply, with big drops in services and construction. Commenting on the figures on 6 January, Markit suggested: "Worryingly, the slide in the PMI all-sector output index from 54.0 in November to 51.4 in December (the largest fall in points terms since November 2008) signals a slowing in GDP growth to near-stagnation in December."

The second chart shows the Nationwide Consumer Confidence Index, which has collapsed since the coalition took office. It now stands at its lowest point since March 2009, and well below its long-run average. The strong rally in sentiment that took place from the middle of 2009 into the first quarter of 2010 has been almost completely reversed. An equivalent EU consumer confidence survey follows a similar path. So much for the improvement in "animal spirits" supposedly brought about by the coalition government's policies.

We see no evidence currently that the UK economy is on course to "liberate new and sustainable investment". Cable agrees, and so do we, that the priority is to get the investment engine restarted. He cites the government's puny "green bank", which is bound to have minimal impact, as it has no money. We need a national investment bank that is committed to spending at least the equivalent of the planned cuts in current spending and ideally more than this. Cuts in payroll taxes – as the US has implemented recently – also look like a sensible way to raise employment.

In short, though Vince Cable's mind is working, the coalition is not.

David Blanchflower is the New Statesman economics editor and a professor at Dartmouth College, New Hampshire, and the University of Stirling

IV. A NATIONAL INVESTMENT BANK

A speech I gave to an investment conference in London on 28 October 2010 (not reproduced here) marked the start of my sustained advocacy of a National Investment Bank. The logic of this was twofold: first, the distinction between capital and current spending, and second, the disappearance of this distinction in the presentation of the public accounts – seen, for example, in the statement that 'government borrowing is deferred taxation'. That is why it seemed to me sensible to set up a separate investment institution to do the borrowing, mandated and capitalized by the government, but constitutionally and operationally independent from it. Although such institutions exist all over the world, and often have an enviable track record in terms of returns on investors' money, the thought of them has become anathema in the UK.

The public finance theory of borrowing was well stated by Thomas Sargent in 1981:

"Before considering the nature of the British deficit in more detail, it helps to remember a few analytical principles about government finance. In interpreting the reported figures on the government's budget deficit, it is useful to keep in mind the hypothetical distinction between "current account" and "capital account" budgets and their deficits. A pure current account expenditure is for a service or perfectly perishable good that gives rise to no government-owned asset that will produce things of value in the future. A pure capital account expenditure is a purchase of a durable asset that gives the government command of a prospective future stream of returns, collected for example through user charges, where the present value is greater than or equal to the present cost of acquiring the asset. A pure capital account budget would count as revenues the interest and other user charges collected on government-owned assets, while expenditures would be purchases of capital assets. On these definitions, government debt issued on capital account is self-liquidating and fully backed by the used charges that are earmarked to pay it off. Government debt issued to finance a pure capital account deficit is thus not a claim on the general tax revenues that the government collects through sales and income taxation. The principles of classical economic theory condone government deficits on capital account."[14]

---

14   Sargent, T. "Stopping moderate inflations: the methods of Poincare and Thatcher", Federal Reserve Board of Minneapolis Research Department Working Paper W, May 1981, pp.23-4

15. A Way out of Britain's Growth Dilemma
Robert Skidelsky and Felix Martin
Financial Times | March 20, 2011

As he prepares for Wednesday's Budget, George Osborne, chancellor, faces a dilemma. On the one hand the recovery has stalled even before his cuts have started. On the other the simple solution of relaxing austerity plans to stave off a double-dip recession is financially and politically unrealistic. Fortunately, there is a way to square this circle – and it requires no U-turn at all.

Mr Osborne dare not renege on plans to liquidate the deficit, fearing (perhaps with good reason) that any change would unsettle the bond markets. But he must also see that, without support, private demand will not suffice to return Britain to full employment. Here the data are clear. In January, the Office for National Statistics revealed that Britain's economy shrank in the fourth quarter of 2010. Recently Jonathan Portes, head of the National Institute for Economic and Social Research, warned in these pages that the first quarter of 2011 looks little better.

What is the best way out of the current dilemma? In his June 2010 emergency Budget Mr Osborne proposed a green investment bank – an idea borrowed from the last Labour administration. In November's spending review, however, the Bank's funding was postponed and made dependent upon privatisation receipts.

The revival and radical scaling-up of this idea can provide a way forward. The chancellor's Budget should expand on existing plans, and consult on establishing a new UK National Investment Bank. This should have a mandate to finance not only "green" projects, but also other that can contribute to the rebalancing of the economy – particularly transport infrastructure, social housing, and export-oriented small and medium-sized enterprises.

There are two main arguments for establishing such a venture. The first is the traditional rationale for public development banks. Private capital markets are prey to short-termism and other market failures, and tend to provide less finance than is optimal to projects that generate economic benefits to the wider economy in excess of their private returns. A public development bank can circumvent these shortcomings by taking a longer-term view, and by including these external benefits in its project appraisals.

This role has long been widely acknowledged in continental Europe and east Asia. However, until recently the conventional view in the UK and US was that a government bank would be bound, for one reason or another, to "pick losers", and thereby pile-up non-performing loans.

But surely only those with a vested interest in denigrating the state will have the nerve to make that argument now, after the catastrophic misjudgments of private banks in the run-up to the crisis.

In any case, like all fundamentalist beliefs, it has little empirical backing. Two relevant comparators – the European Investment Bank, and Germany's Kreditanstalt für Wiederaufbau – show that, in well-regulated financial systems, such banks pay for themselves.

But it is a second argument that should clinch Mr Osborne's decision now: a national investment bank could play a significant role in short run stabilisation too. A limited fiscal commitment – say, £10bn in subscribed capital, with contributions drawn down over the next four years – would allow the new bank to finance enough spending to more than offset the £87bn of reductions in public investment planned before 2015. In this way it could provide a way to bolster confidence and increase demand, without adding significantly to the deficit.

The difference between the total and government contribution would be funded from the bond markets. This is the magic of leverage, of course: that magic which got such a black name as a cause of the crisis. But a national investment bank is an opportunity to turn that magic to a constructive end.

In fact, an investment bank would kill three birds with one stone. First, through its funding programme, it would create a new class of bonds – long term, but with a yield pick-up over gilts, reflecting the modest credit risk of the Bank – which could include features that fit the needs of the UK pensions industry, as the population ages. Second, by lending for the long term, and in line with economic and environmental priorities, it would help long-term growth. And finally by ramping up its operations now – when the corporate recovery is being hamstrung by shrinking bank lending and fiscal austerity – it can offer a boost to aggregate demand when it is needed most.

The only question likely to be asked of Mr Osborne is why he has to create a new public bank, when the state owns two already. A fair question: but then this bank will also be setting out to prove that banking does not have to be, in Lord Turner's scathing rebuke, "socially useless". For that it may be better to start with a clean slate.

Felix Martin is an investment analyst at Thames River Capital

16. Lord Speaker's Economics Seminar
House of Lords | June 15, 2011

Since 2008 we have experienced a financial crisis and a fiscal crisis. The two are connected by the shrinkage of the economy and the concomitant expansion of the budget deficit. It's simply not true that the large budget deficit this government inherited was largely the result of the fiscal extravagance of the last government. It was largely due to the scale of the collapse of a structurally weak economy. This explains why the structural deficit is so large.

I don't think anyone here would absolve the last government of all blame. I think it was culpable in two respects: first, it accepted too readily that a systemic collapse of the banking sector was impossible, owing to risk diversification. It therefore based its fiscal projections on the continued prosperity of the financial sector. Secondly, it bought into the idea that the financial sector was the growth engine of the British economy. The City of London became its fetish.

It seems odd that a Labour government should have accepted so uncritically what was originally a Thatcherite idea. A historian will have to explain why. But be that as it may, the government made no real attempt to achieve a balanced private economy. One result of this was that a large part of the labour released from the continuing decline of manufacturing was absorbed into an expanding public sector.

Having said this, I believe that the present government has pursued completely the wrong macroeconomic policy, and this explains why the British recovery, together with that of certain other peripheral European states, is in the slow lane of the world recovery.

The Chancellor's strategy is very easy to understand, as he has so often explained it. If the government offers a credible deficit reduction programme, chiefly by cutting spending, this will create the confidence needed to unleash a private investment boom. A subsidiary argument, particularly important in June 2010, was that unless the new government got the public finances under firm control, Britain would go the way of Greece – that is, the cost of its debt would rise towards the Greek level.

I don't want to discuss the second argument, except to say that if Opposition politicians continually talk down the financial policy of the government they are hoping to replace, markets may come to believe them. Recovery hinges on the first argument being true, and I would claim that it is false on straightforward Keynesian grounds. If the public sector and private sector are increasing their saving simultaneously, there will be a fall in domestic aggregate demand and this will cause output and employment to be lower than they would have been. It will also, ironically, cause the deficit to be larger than it would have been. I think we already have some confirmation of this hypothesis in the slowdown in recovery and the higher than projected rise in the deficit.

I don't believe that there is any solid empirical support for the theory of expansionary fiscal contraction (as it's fashionably called). Evidence from both the Swedish experience of 1994 and the Thatcher government's record of 1981-2 shows that the depressive effects of contractionary fiscal policy may be offset by expansionary monetary policy and/or a fall in the exchange rate. But it would be more natural to ascribe recovery in such circumstances to one or other of these two factors than to the fiscal contraction. And I have no need to remind those present that, despite the rapid recovery from the slump, unemployment continued to rise for five years, peaking at 3m in 1986. I believe that Britain was permanently scarred by that experience.

This brings me to Plan B. We have already had some relief from the quantitative easing programme of 2009-10, which pumped £200bn into the banking system, and from a 21 per cent depreciation of sterling against a trade weighted currency index since early 2008. Most of this depreciation occurred in 2008, so we have already had most of its benefits. I think we will have to have another bout of QE before the year is out. But I don't think it will suffice to bring about vigorous recovery. On monetary policy, all I will do is to repeat Keynes's graphic phrase: 'If...we are tempted to assert that money is the drink which stimulates the economy to activity, we must remind ourselves that there may be several slips between the cup and the lip'.[15] All the uncertainties of QE lie in that single phrase.

So it may soon be time for Plan C. I have been arguing for a National Investment Bank, with a mandate to invest in green projects, transport infrastructure, social housing and export-oriented SMEs. A limited fiscal commitment of say £10bn over four years would allow the new bank to spend, say, £100bn with conservative gearing. The Chancellor has taken a small step in this direction by accepting the last government's proposal for a Green Bank –but it will only be allowed to spend £3bn, and can only start borrowing in 2015 after the structural deficit has gone. Since I don't believe it will have gone by then, the scheme will need to be drastically re-thought if it's to do any good.

A principal merit of this idea is that such a bank could create a new class of bonds – long-term but with a slightly higher yield than gilts, which would suit long-term investors, like pension funds, while offering loans at slightly below the commercial rate. For those whose instinctive reaction is that such a bank would be bound to back losers,

15   JMK, *General Theory*, p. 173

I recommend Michael Litovksy's *Obama's Bank*, a careful study of how such institutions have worked in the United States. They can be made to work, and may be indispensable if there's no other way to draw out frozen private savings.

17. Osborne needs a Plan C
The Guardian | June 21, 2011

George Osborne expected to inherit a booming economy. In September 2007 – the month Northern Rock collapsed – he promised to match Labour's spending plans for his first three years as chancellor. He said that because the economy was set to grow faster than projected government spending, this would leave the Conservatives room for tax cuts. It is worth recalling this pledge in the light of the later Conservative charge that Gordon Brown ruined the economy. In 2007 both parties shared the same rosy growth expectations, and differed only on the question of how to divide the medium term spoils between tax cuts and public spending.

In fact, George Osborne unexpectedly inherited an economy ruined by the great global contraction which started in 2008. When he became Chancellor the British economy had shrunk by 5.5 per cent from its pre-recession peak, and the budget deficit had risen from 2.5 per cent of GDP to 10 per cent, the second being a counterpart of the first. But it also soon became conventional to say that the Labour government's revenue projections had been based on quite unrealistic growth expectations, and that therefore the 'structural deficit' – that bit of the deficit not due to the downturn – was nearer 8 per cent than 2.5 per cent. There some truth in this. But, pre-crash, the Conservatives did not challenge Labour's revenue estimates. Osborne and Alastair Darling were equally fooled by the brittle buoyancy of the British economy.

The British economy started to recover from the recession in the last quarter of 2009. This recovery had nothing to do with the cuts, because they had not happened. The two most likely causes were the 21 per cent depreciation of sterling against competitor currencies, and a £200bn injection of cash into the banking system, starting in February 2009. However, there is no golden light at the end of the tunnel.

Broadly speaking, we are bouncing along the bottom, with growth expected to slow down, not to speed up. It is still way below the trend growth rate of 2.5 per cent a year. Unemployment has remained flat at 7.7 per cent. Bank lending to British businesses contracted by 4.3 per cent in twelve months to February 2011, and the effective rate on new mortgage lending, at 3.85 per cent, was exactly the same as it was at the beginning of 2010. The FTSE 100 index is the same as it was just before the election. Britain is very much in the slow lane of global recovery, and this is all before the cuts have started to bite.

In 2010, both Darling and Osborne produced deficit reduction plans, mainly through spending cuts. The Labour chancellor Alastair Darling promised to take £73bn out of the economy in four years, Osborne to take out £112bn over the same period. But the cuts proper would only start in April 2011. Osborne claimed that his tighter reduction plan was necessary to restore the confidence of the markets – which by June 2010 were reeling from the Greek crisis. The important point to note is that in Osborne's first year the bulk of public spending remained largely untouched. So far his Iron Chancellorship has been rhetorical. The extra pain is yet to come.

What will be the effect of reducing the deficit by £112bn in the next four years? The Osborne theory is that any reduction in government borrowing is equivalent to transferring spending power to the private sector. The private sector will have £83bn more (£112bn minus the £29bn in higher taxes) – to spend – to consume and invest. Workers released from the public sector will be absorbed in private sector jobs. Since private spending is more profitable than public spending and since, in addition, the tighter Conservative deficit reduction programme will boost confidence in the economy, the result will be a net increase in aggregate demand, and a higher growth rate. Fiscal contraction is the royal road to buoyant recovery.

The Keynesian view is the exact opposite. Taking £112bn out of the economy will be a net subtraction from aggregate demand. The £83bn cuts in public spending will not be matched by an equivalent increase in private spending because their first effect will be to reduce employment, and hence reduce the national income. (The newly unemployed will have less income than before). So part of the money the government 'saves' will simply disappear as the national income shrinks. Fiscal contraction is the royal road to stagnation, not recovery.

These two theories are about to be tested. The Keynesians – among whom I number myself – will have to eat their words if growth picks up, and unemployment falls in the next twelve months, as £32bn is subtracted from the economy in taxes and spending cuts. Osborne should eat his words if there is no improvement in growth and employment, but he almost certainly won't. If things fail to go his way, he will claim that a sound strategy was 'blown off course' by unforeseen events. Politicians always claim that it is the world which is wrong, not their policy.

Nevertheless, even the Chancellor will find it prudent to have Plan B up his sleeve if the economy continues to stagnate. (Though of course he will never admit to having it).Most analysts expect Plan B to be another bout of the 'quantitative easing' which helped stabilized the economy in 2009-10. So, despite the sharp, but probably temporary spike in inflation, I would expect the Bank to try again.

But monetary policy is a very uncertain instrument. It's not the printing of money, but the spending of money that is important for recovery, and printing money does not ensure that it is spent, if the public is not in a spending mood. As Keynes graphically put it: 'If… we are tempted to assert that money is the drink which stimulates the economy to activity, we must remind ourselves that there may be several slips between the cup and the lip'.

That is why we may need a Plan C. I have been advocating a National Investment Bank, with a mandate to invest in green projects, transport infrastructure, social housing, and export-oriented businesses. A limited fiscal commitment of say £10bn over four years would allow the bank to spend say £100bn with conservative gearing. It would create a new class of bonds with a slightly higher yield than gilts, which would suit long-term investors like pension funds, while offering loans at slightly below the commercial rates. The Chancellor already possesses the necessary instrument in the Green Bank, but with a meagre capitalisation of £3bn and no borrowing power, it cannot do any good over the period of the cuts.

An investment bank of the kind I am suggesting would enable the Chancellor to continue to preach public austerity while silently undermining its depressive effects. And who could ask better than that?

18. Osborne's austerity gamble is fast being found out
Robert Skidelsky and Felix Martin
Financial Times | July 31, 2011

George Osborne is fond of martial metaphors. In his Mansion House speech in June, the Chancellor quoted Winston Churchill in support of his deficit reduction plan: "Now this is not the end. It is not even the beginning of the end. But it is, perhaps, the end of the beginning." But at 0.2 per cent, growth in the second quarter has once again cast doubt on Mr Osborne's boast that his strategy is working. A quote from Tacitus would have been better: "They made a wasteland and called it peace."

The reason the current strategy will fail was succinctly stated by John Maynard Keynes. Growth depends on aggregate demand. If you reduce aggregate demand, you reduce growth. This is what is happening.

When he assumed office in May 2010, the Chancellor claimed Britain's government faced a loss of investor confidence that demanded fiscal retrenchment. The initial reaction to his emergency Budget of June 2010 was favourable: on the markets gilt yields fell and Mr Osborne basked in the approval of the International Monetary Fund.

Yet these two crucial pillars of support for the coalition's policy look shaky. First, the international technocrats now seem much less certain that the Chancellor is leading us out of recession. In its latest and most sophisticated study of fiscal austerity, the IMF concluded that it did have "contractionary effects on private domestic demand and GDP".

This should hardly come as a surprise: IMF studies from 2009 and 2010 found the same. Potentially much more destructive, however, investors are also beginning to change their tune.

In the early days of the Eurozone sovereign debt crisis the markets did indeed identify fiscal profligacy as the problem. Investors demanded an austerity plan in Greece, and were delivered one in May 2010. The results have disappointed, however – with the continued shrinkage of the Greek economy leading to missed fiscal targets, despite aggressive cuts. Last month, the original bail-out programme had to be extended, as investors continued to flee Greek bonds.

When, in July, the crisis spread to Italy, many analysts were puzzled. Why should the only Eurozone country scheduled to run a primary fiscal surplus in 2011 be under attack? The message from the bond markets is clear: investors have begun to realise that austerity alone is proving a false trail. The royal road to creditworthiness runs not via cuts alone, but via growth.

These recent bond market developments should worry the Chancellor. His one-dimensional focus on austerity was once the government's greatest asset. It is fast becoming its major liability.

Fortunately, he already has the tools he needs to change course.

As we have argued, a scaling-up of the government's new Green Investment Bank – to become a full-scale National Investment Bank – can play a major role. Keynes advocated digging holes and filling them up again if the government could think of nothing better to do. But the coalition has already identified a more useful range of investments – like halving carbon emissions from 1990 levels by 2025.

The obstacle so far has been funding: the Treasury has provided the Green Investment Bank with only £3bn of capital and will not allow it to borrow. Yet here too the coalition is already close to a solution. Nick Clegg, deputy prime minister, recently began a debate over how to dispose of the government's shareholdings in the UK's bailed-out banks. Rather than his plan to distribute shares to voters, the government should use the proceeds of selling its stock to capitalise a full National Investment Bank.

This would be neutral for public debt and require no new deficit spending. With (say) £10bn and the power to borrow, the enlarged bank could begin to mobilise frozen private savings to offset the effects of fiscal contraction, while also preparing the economy for a greener future. This would not be a Plan B or even Plan C. Instead it would be Plan A+, to which all sides ought to be able to agree.

19. The Wages of Economic Ignorance
Project Syndicate | November 21, 2011

Politicians are masters at "passing the buck." Everything good that happens reflects their exceptional talents and efforts; everything bad is caused by someone or something else.

The economy is a classic field for this strategy. Three years after the global economy's near-collapse, the feeble recovery has already petered out in most developed countries, whose economic inertia will drag down the rest. Pundits discern a "double-dip" recession, but in some countries the first dip never ended: Greek GDP has been dipping for three years.

When we ask politicians to explain these deplorable results, they reply in unison: "It's not our fault." Recovery, goes the refrain, has been "derailed" by the eurozone crisis. But this is to turn the matter on its head. The eurozone crisis did not derail recovery; it is the result of a lack of recovery. It is the natural, predictable, and (by many) predicted result of the main European countries' deliberate policy of repressing aggregate demand.

That policy was destined to produce a financial crisis, because it was bound to leave governments and banks with depleted assets and larger debts. Despite austerity, the forecast of this year's UK structural deficit has increased from 6.5 per cent to 8 per cent – requiring an extra £22 billion ($34.6 billion) in cuts a year. Prime Minister David Cameron and Chancellor George Osborne blame the eurozone crisis; in fact, their own economic illiteracy is to blame.

Unfortunately for all of us, the true explanation bears repeating nowadays. Depressions, recessions, contractions – call them what you will – occur because the private-sector spends less than it did previously. This means that its income falls, because spending by one firm or household is income for another.

In this situation, government deficits rise naturally, as tax revenues decline and spending on unemployment insurance and other benefits rises. These "automatic stabilizers" plug part of the private-sector spending gap.

But if the government starts reducing its own deficit before private-sector spending recovers, the net result will be a further decline in total spending, and hence in total income, causing the government's deficit to widen, rather than narrow. True, if governments stop spending altogether, deficits will eventually fall to zero. People will starve to death, but the budget will be balanced.

That is the crazy logic of current economic policy in much of Europe (and elsewhere). Of course, it will not be carried through to the bitter end. Too much will crack along the way – the banks, the monetary system, social cohesion, the legitimacy of the political regime. Our leaders may be intellectually challenged, but they are not suicidal. Deficit reduction eventually will be put into cold storage, either openly, as I would prefer, or surreptitiously, as is politicians' way. In the United Kingdom, there is already talk of Plan A +.

Those who see the need for such a growth strategy, but who also want to help their friends, like the idea of tax cuts – especially for the rich. This knocks a hole in current deficit-reduction plans, but, provided government continues to cut spending, it has the benefit (from a conservative's point of view) of shrinking the state's role over time.

Apart from questions of fairness, cutting top tax rates is an inferior way to increase spending, because the rich have a higher propensity to save. Tax reductions should be targeted specifically at the poor if one wants the money to be spent to stimulate the economy.

In fact, the best option of all is for the government to spend the money itself. Governments can do this consistently with a medium-term deficit-reduction plan by making a crucial distinction between their budgets' current and capital accounts. The current account covers spending on services and perishable goods that produce no assets. The capital account is for buying or building durable assets that give a prospective future return. The first is a charge on taxation; the second is not.

If today's accounting rules are too insensitive to make this distinction, a separate entity could do the investing. A national investment bank would be capitalized by the government, borrow from the private sector, and invest in infrastructure, housing, and "greening" the economy. This would simultaneously plug a hole in demand and improve the economy's long-term growth prospects. There are signs that officials in the UK and the United States are starting to move in this direction.

If nothing works, it will be time to sprinkle the country with what Milton Friedman called "helicopter money" – that is, put purchasing power directly into people's pockets, by giving every household a spending voucher with an expiration date. This would at least keep the economy afloat pending the development of the longer-term investment program.

It would be better if recovery plans could be agreed upon by all by G-20 countries, as was briefly the case in the coordinated stimulus of April 2009. If not, groups of countries should pursue them on their own.

The European Union desperately needs a growth strategy. Its current bailout schemes only help countries like Greece and Italy to borrow money cheaply in the face of prohibitively high market interest rates, while the schemes' insistence on more budget-deficit reduction in these countries will reduce European purchasing power further. The recipient governments will have to cut their spending; the banks will have to take large losses.

In the long run, the eurozone must be recognized as a failed experiment. It should be reconstituted with far fewer members, including only countries that do not run persistent current-account deficits. Everything else that has been proposed to save the eurozone in its current form – a central treasury, a monetary authority that does more than target inflation, fiscal harmonization, a new treaty – is a political pipe dream.

20. Twixt' cup and lip: the flaw in quantitative easing

Robert Skidelsky and Felix Martin
Financial Times | November 23, 2011

The Office for Budget Responsibility forecast in March that the UK economy would grow by 1.7 per cent in 2011, and that the government could meet its target of eliminating the structural deficit by 2014-15. But the economy has underperformed these forecasts by so much that it now seems growth will be little more than 1 per cent, and the target not achieved until 2016-17. A recent speech by David Cameron showed he was preparing to announce what a report from Barclays Capital neatly called "two years' slippage in eight months".

So we have embarked on Plan B – printing money, though only to a modest extent, a £75bn programme of "quantitative easing" announced by the Bank of England on 6th October. For those who never believed in Plan A – chancellor George Osborne's original view that cutting public spending would automatically produce economic recovery – resort to monetary policy is the start of a more interesting debate, about whether monetary policy alone can engineer a recovery from recession.

Milton Friedman said yes, arguing that it was the Fed's failure in 1930 to pursue "open market operations" on the scale needed that deepened the slump. Against this view is Keynes's famous retort: "If, however, we are tempted to assert that money is the drink which stimulates the system to activity, we must remind ourselves that there may be several slips between cup and lip." Keynes postulated two possible slips.

Firstly, monetary policy may not succeed in reducing the interest rates faced by borrowers. The relevant interest rate is of course the risky interest rate faced by corporate borrowers – not the risk-free gilt yield. So the question is whether QE will reduce not only gilt yields but also the risky interest rate.

Secondly, lower interest rates may not stimulate growth in lending and economic activity. This is a question of demand – even with a lower risky interest rate, will demand for borrowing increase? This is the only channel whereby the interest rate can drive spending.

So how did the first round of quantitative easing, which pumped £200m into the economy between March 2009 and February 2010 fare on these two counts? The Bank has just published its own assessment.

On interest rates, it concludes that QE was effective in reducing risk-free interest rates (gilt yields). However, even for the very few companies that can borrow in the bond markets, the effect on the interest rate faced by investment grade companies over and above this was virtually non-existent. The net result was a very modest reduction in the interest rate they faced (of around 0.7 per cent), which was dwarfed by changes driven by the evolving macroeconomic picture.

For the majority of companies that can only borrow from banks, even this small victory was absent. The Bank reported "little evidence that effective new bank lending rates for households or firms fell significantly following QE purchases".

On the second slip, the evidence is pretty damning. Lending to private non-financial companies has fallen by more than 12 per cent since QE1 began in March 2009, and lending to small and medium sized enterprises has been even harder hit.

There are two reasons for the two slips. Risky interest rates remain stubbornly high. The banking sector is broken and is not transmitting monetary policy through to borrowers. And borrowing is shrinking for two reasons: over-indebted households and companies do not want to borrow at any interest rate. Among those that are not over-indebted, confidence is shattered – uncertainty is so high that few want to put capital at risk.

The verdict is already in. Indeed, the Bank's governor has given it on countless occasions: monetary policy cannot save the economy. Seriously negative interest rates might work – but only at the cost of debauching the currency, which is the last refuge of a desperate government. Since the governor rejects both this and fiscal stimulus, his only remedy seems to be to grin and bear it until the global economy is set to rights.

The most terrifying thing to emerge from the Bank of England's reports is that the Bank embarked on its experiment without any macro-economic model specifying how money was to be transmitted to income. In other words, QE was launched on a wing and prayer.

So it is up to the politicians to rescue the economy from years of stagnation. As I have said before, we urgently need a Plan C: a strategy for investment and growth. The chancellor will have a chance to unveil one in his pre-budget statement of 29 November. But will he have an ace up his sleeve?

21. Autumn statement: George Osborne's cutting fantasy is over
The Guardian | Tuesday, November 29, 2011

In his autumn statement today the chancellor claimed it was his deficit reduction plan that enabled the British government to borrow money even more cheaply than the Germans, thus saving the taxpayer £21bn in interest rate charges over five years. Ed Balls rejoined that "he still clings to the illiterate fantasy that low long-term interest rates in Britain are a sign of enhanced credibility and not, as they were in Japan in the 1990s or in America today, a sign of stagnant growth in our economy". The intellectual debate between George Osborne and his critics hinges on this single point: what is it that makes a deficit-reduction programme "credible"?

Let's start with the theory of the matter. "Look after unemployment," Keynes said, "and the budget will look after itself." This was a neat way of saying that a credible deficit reduction plan depends on growth. All governments have large deficits at present because their economies have shrunk. The deficits will decline automatically as their economies start growing.

But policies of deficit reduction will not in themselves produce growth. Nor will they eliminate the deficit. Trying to reduce the deficit by cutting spending and raising taxes means taking spending power out of the economy, when what a depressed economy needs is more spending. A government can always cut its own spending. But it cannot control its income. If cutting its spending leads to a fall in its revenue, it is little nearer "balancing the books" than before. One person's spending is another's income. If the government reduces the economy's spending, its own income will fall.

This grisly truth is at last starting to pierce the fog of rhetoric. The latest report of the Office for Budget Responsibility predicts that the government will miss its borrowing target this year because of reduced revenues. Even though it has cut spending by more than its goal, the fall in tax revenues – £15bn less than expected this year – has knocked it off target.

The economy has hardly grown for a year and, says the OECD, is now likely to contract. Lower growth over the next five years means the government will have to borrow £111bn more than planned. The brief recovery is over. The shrinkage in demand is becoming a collapse. Unemployment will still be rising in 2013, real wages will continue to decline and as households stop spending, company profits will suffer. The deficit will not be gone by 2015. Even to get rid of it by 2017 – the latest estimate – will require a further £23bn of cuts. But as these will reduce growth even further, the elimination of the deficit can safely be postponed to never-never land.

We come to the question of confidence. The chancellor has repeatedly claimed that the deficit reduction programme was, and is, necessary to maintain investor confidence in government finances. Confidence is very important, but also mysterious: the bond markets can believe a dozen contradictory things before breakfast. The main point is that confidence cannot be separated from the economy's performance. As it stalls, the creditworthiness of governments declines as their debt increases, raising the likelihood of default.

A year ago bond traders, having forgotten what little economic theory they knew, were inclined to believe that deficit reduction would in itself generate recovery. For several months the Osbornites fed them the fantasy of "expansionary fiscal contraction", the idea that as the deficit falls the economy would expand. This story is now exploded. It's the economy that determines the size of the deficit, not the deficit that determines the size of the economy.

The chancellor is right to say that Britain is not at the "centre of the sovereign debt storm". But for how much longer? The eurozone financial crisis – on both its sovereign and commercial bank sides – is the direct result of policies which have brought about the slowdown of the European economies. From August to September industrial production turned sharply downwards in the EU, and especially the eurozone. But our government has been pursuing the same policies, with the same results. This suggests that, without a change of policy, the price of our own government debt will start to go up.

I agree, therefore, with Ed Balls. The government's debt-reduction strategy is not credible, either as theory, or in terms of maintaining the markets' confidence. The chancellor's plan would have looked good had it worked. It has fallen so far short of it that Osborne sees the need to introduce a subplot into the main narrative. This goes under the name of "credit easing".

He has authorised the Bank of England to buy an extra £75bn worth of government bonds – known as "quantitative easing" – to increase the reserves of the banking system. Banks will be given government guarantees to raise money more cheaply provided they lend to small and medium-sized businesses. The government will offer to secure part of the loans taken out by first-time buyers of new-build homes, enabling them to get larger mortgages with a smaller deposit at lower interest rates. The government also intends to "mobilise the finance" for an infrastructure programme, though how it can get the pension funds on board without subsidised interest rates and/or guaranteed income streams is not clear. These are steps in the right direction. But, according to the OBR: "It is far from clear how much additional lending [credit easing] will create."

What the chancellor is trying to do is to increase the supply of credit. But the austerity side of his policy is choking off the demand for credit by reducing the size of the market. The new policy is therefore incoherent. What we need is not a subplot but a new narrative, which recognises that the most important requirement for recovery is to increase total spending in the economy. In this story, increasing capital spending is the main plot, cutting current spending the subplot. The chancellor is edging towards this, but he has not arrived. Events may force the pace.

V. PEERING INTO THE FUTURE

The next four items are more general. The first two deal with the problems of social democracy. The third is an argument for the rebalancing of the British economy away from finance. The fourth looks at the prospects for globalization. More extensive treatments of these themes can be found on my website www.skidelskyr.com

22. Keynes and Social Democracy Today
Project Syndicate I June 22, 2010

For decades, Keynesianism was associated with social democratic big-government policies. But John Maynard Keynes's relationship with social democracy is complex. Although he was an architect of core components of social democratic policy – particularly its emphasis on maintaining full employment – he did not subscribe to other key social democratic objectives, such as public ownership or massive expansion of the welfare state.

In *The General Theory of Employment, Interest and Money*, Keynes ends by summarizing the strengths and weaknesses of the capitalist system. On one hand, capitalism offers the best safeguard of individual freedom, choice, and entrepreneurial initiative. On the other hand, unregulated markets fail to achieve two central goals of any civilized society: "The outstanding faults of the economic society in which we live are its failure to provide for full employment and its arbitrary and inequitable distribution of wealth and incomes." This suggested an active role for government, which dovetailed with important strands of left-wing thought.

Until the *General Theory* was published in 1936, social democrats did not know how to go about achieving full employment. Their policies were directed at depriving capitalists of the ownership of the means of production. How this was to produce full employment was never worked out.

There was an idea, originally derived from Ricardo and Marx, that the capitalist class needed a "reserve army of the unemployed" to maintain its profit share. If profits were eliminated, the need for that reserve army would disappear. Labour would be paid what it was worth, and everyone willing to work would be able to find a job.

But, apart from the political impossibility of nationalizing the whole economy peacefully, this approach suffered from the fatal flaw of ignoring the role of aggregate demand. It assumed that demand would always be sufficient if profits were eliminated.

Keynes demonstrated that the main cause of bouts of heavy and prolonged unemployment was not worker encroachment on profits, but the fluctuating prospects of private investment in an uncertain world. Nearly all unemployment in a cyclical downturn was the result of the failure of investment demand.

Thus, the important thing was not to nationalize the capital stock, but to socialize investment. Industry could be safely left in private hands, provided the state guaranteed enough spending power in the economy to maintain a full-employment level of investment. This could be achieved by monetary and fiscal policy: low interest rates and large state investment programs.

In short, Keynes aimed to achieve a key social democratic objective without changing the ownership of industry. Nevertheless, he did think that redistribution would help secure full employment. A greater tendency to consume would "serve to increase at the same time the inducement to invest." And the low interest rates needed to maintain full employment would lead in time to the "euthanasia of the rentier" – of those who live off the rents of capital.

Moderate re-distribution was the more politically radical implication of Keynes's economic theory, but the measures outlined above were also the limits of state intervention for him. As long as "the state is able to determine the aggregate amount of resources devoted to augmenting the instruments [i.e., the capital base] and the basic reward to those who own them," there is no "obvious case" for further involvement. The public was never to substitute for the private, but merely to complement it.

Today, ideas about full employment and equality remain at the heart of social democracy. But the political struggle needs to be conducted along new battle lines. Whereas the front used to run between government and the owners of the means of production – the industrialists, the rentiers – now, it runs between governments and finance. Such measures as the efforts by the European Parliament to regulate the derivatives market or the British government's ban on short selling in the wake of the financial crisis or the demand to cap bankers' bonuses are contemporary expressions of the wish to reduce the power of financial speculation to damage the economy.

The new focus on the need to tame the power of finance is largely a consequence of globalization. Capital moves across borders more freely and more quickly than goods or people do. Yet, while large global firms habitually use their high concentration of financial resources to press for further de-regulation ("or we will go somewhere else"), the crisis has turned their size into a liability.

Being too big to fail simply means being too big. Keynes saw that "it is the financial markets' precariousness which creates no small part of our contemporary problem of securing sufficient investment." That rings truer today – more than 70 years later – than in his own day. Rather than securing investment for productive sectors of the economy, the financial industry has become adept at securing investment in itself.

This, once again, calls for an activist government policy. Yet, as Keynes would have argued, it is important that the expansion of government involvement is informed by sound economics rather than political ideology, social democratic or otherwise.

State intervention needs to bridge gaps that the private sector cannot reasonably be expected to do on its own. The current crisis has shown with utmost clarity that private markets are unable to self-regulate; domestic regulation is therefore a key area in which government has a role to play. Similarly, time-inconsistency issues prevent large international firms from compartmentalizing their markets. Re-erecting barriers to capital flows in the form of international taxes, thereby cordoning off crises before they turn global, is therefore another task for government.

Keynes's main contribution to social democracy, however, does not lie in the specifics of policy, but in his insistence that the state as ultimate protector of the public good has a duty to supplement and regulate market forces. If we need markets to stop the state from behaving badly, we need the state to stop markets from behaving badly. Nowadays, that means stopping financial markets from behaving badly. That means limiting their power, and their profits.

23. Recovery Before Reform

Project Syndicate | October 20, 2011

The financial crisis that started in 2007 shrunk the world economy by 6 per cent in two years, doubling unemployment. Its proximate cause was predatory bank lending, so people are naturally angry and want heads and bonuses to roll – a sentiment captured by the current worldwide protests against "Wall Street."

The banks, however, are not just part of the problem, but an essential part of the solution. The same institutions that caused the crisis must help to solve it, by starting to lend again. With global demand flagging, the priority has to be recovery, without abandoning the goal of reform – a difficult line to tread politically.

The common ground of reform is the need to re-regulate the financial services industry. In the run-up to the crisis, experts loudly claimed that "efficient" financial markets could be safely left to regulate themselves. Reflecting the freebooting financial zeitgeist that prevailed at the time, the International Monetary Fund declared in 2006 that "the dispersion of credit risk by banks to a broader and more diverse group of investors...has helped make the banking and overall financial system more resilient..." As a result, "the commercial banks may be less vulnerable to...shocks."

It is impossible not to hear in such nonsense the cocksure drumbeat of the Money Power, which has never failed to identify the public interest with its own. For 50 years after the Great Depression of the 1930s, the Money Power was held to account by the countervailing power of government. At the heart of the political check was America's Glass-Steagall Act of 1933.

Glass-Steagall aimed to prevent commercial banks from gambling with their depositors' money by mandating the institutional separation of retail and investment banking. The result was 65 years of relative financial stability. In what economists later called the "repressed" financial system, retail banks fulfilled the necessary function of financial intermediation without taking on suicidal risks, while the government kept aggregate demand high enough to maintain a full-employment level of investment.

Then the Money Power struck back, aided and abetted by its apologist cohort of economists. The Big Bang of 1986 in London ended the separation of banking functions in the United Kingdom. After prolonged lobbying by the financial-services industry, US President Bill Clinton repealed Glass-Steagall in 1999. From that point on, commercial and investment banks could merge, and the composite entities were authorized to provide a full range of banking services, including underwriting and other trading activities.

This was part of a wave of deregulation that swept away Franklin Roosevelt's promise to "chase the money changers from the temple." Clinton also refused to regulate credit-default swaps, and the US Securities and Exchange Commission allowed banks to triple their leverage. These three decisions led directly to the sub-prime extravaganza that brought down the US banking system in 2007-2008.

Since that crash, efforts have been made to reconstruct the dismantled system of financial regulation in order to prevent the "over-lending" that led to the collapse. The new doctrine is called "macro-prudential regulation." Under an international agreement known as Basel III, banks are to be required to hold a higher ratio of equity capital against "risk-weighted assets," and leverage is to be limited to a smaller percentage of such assets. National regulators are exploring ways to vary ratio requirements over the business cycle, and have started subjecting banks to regular "stress tests."

In the UK, a Financial Policy Committee within the Bank of England is to monitor the "systemic risk" of financial failure, with a Prudential Regulatory Authority supervising systemically important institutions. According to monetary economist Charles Goodhart, a significantly faster-than-normal growth rate for bank credit, house prices, and leverage will give the authorities sufficient warning of impending crisis.

The new orthodoxy places its faith in regulators' ability to improve on banks' measurement of risk, while leaving the structure of the banking system unchanged. But, when it comes to upping equity requirements against "risk-weighted assets," who is to do the weighting, and according to what methodology?

Goodhart concedes that banks' "risk weightings" in the pre-recession period were subject to political pressure and "financial-industry capture and manipulation." This is inevitable, because, as John Maynard Keynes pointed out, the "riskiness" of many investments, being subject to inherent uncertainty, is immeasurable. In short, the new regulatory philosophy replaces the illusion that banks can safely be left to manage their risks with the illusion that regulators will do it for them.

Meanwhile, initial enthusiasm for restoring Glass-Steagall – breaking up banking functions into separate institutions – has fallen by the wayside. It is only logical that banks with state-guaranteed deposits should be safe and boring, with other necessary, but risky activities hived off to separate companies. But little progress has been made in (re)implementing this idea.

The "Volcker rule," whereby commercial banks would be barred from trading on their own account, and from owning hedge funds and private-equity firms, languishes in Congress. In the UK, an Independent

Commission on Banking, headed by Sir John Vickers, rejected separation of retail from investment banking, recommending instead "ring-fencing" deposits from the investment arms of universal banks.

Trust-busters argue that such "Chinese walls" always break down under pressure, owing to huge shareholder demand for universal banks to boost profits at the expense of a sound commercial banking core. And senior executives will still have a legal obligation to maximize profits. The Vickers commission's proposals also depend on sophisticated regulation, which assumes, against history, that regulators will always be one step ahead of bankers.

The Money Power never surrenders easily. Whether relying on regulation, or gesturing towards institutional separation, most proposals for banking reform remain at the drawing-board stage, and are sure to be emasculated by financial lobbies.

Moreover, whatever their intrinsic merits, none of these proposals addresses the global economy's most immediate problem: undersupply, not oversupply, of credit. In other words, the challenge is to revive lending growth in full awareness that we must begin devising ways to rein it in.

24. The case for a balanced economy reconsidered
Speech to New Political Economy Network I June 27, 2011

What I want to do today is to reconsider the case for a balanced economy.

In one sense this has nothing to do with Keynes. As you know, his *General Theory* offered a short-run model of employment, in which the existing structure of the economy was taken as given. The task was simply to increase aggregate demand: the distribution of demand was not in the remit.

However, Keynes did have views on the structure of the economy, which come out most strongly in 1933, especially in his 'National Self-Sufficiency' articles of 1933. One can interpret his ideas here as 'second best' arguments for a world in which international trade had collapsed. But they are more positive than that. Take first, his remark: 'Let Goods be Homespun':

> 'I am not persuaded that the economic advantages of the international division of labour to-day are at all comparable with what they were… Experience accumulates to prove that most modern mass-production processes can be performed in most countries and climates with almost equal efficiency…Moreover, as wealth increases, both primary and manufactured products play a smaller relative part in the national economy compared with houses, personal services, and local amenities which are not the subject of international exchange…[16]

Consider second, 'Let finance be primarily national'. Keynes always claimed that domestic investment was better than foreign investment, because less riskier 'To lend vast sums abroad for long periods of time without any possibility of legal redress if things go wrong, is a crazy construction; especially in return for a trifling extra interest'[17]. He wrote in 1924: 'With home investment, even if it be ill-advised or extravagantly carried out, at least the country has the improvement for what it is worth. The worst conceived and most extravagant housing scheme imaginable leaves us with some houses. A bad foreign investment is wholly engulfed'.[18]

A third strand in the National Self-Sufficiency argument concerns political economy. National self-sufficiency promised a 'well-balanced' or 'complete' national life, allowing the British to display the full range

16   JMK, Collected Works, xxi, p.238
17   JMK, CW, xix, p.278
18   JMK, 'Foreign Investment and National Advantage', 9 August 1924, in CW, xix, pp. 278,83

of their national aptitudes in mechanical invention and in agriculture, as well as preserving traditional ways of living. If all this domestic activity cost the consumer a bit more, so be it. 'To say that the country cannot afford agriculture is to delude oneself about the meaning of the word 'afford'. A country which cannot afford art or agriculture, invention or tradition, is a country in which one cannot afford to live'. Keynes also paid homage to localism: he wanted towns in which 'shops are really shops and not merely a branch of the multiplication table'.

Finally, Keynes stressed the value of national independence:

> 'We each have our own fancy. Not believing we are saved already, we each would like to have a try at working out our salvation. We do not wish, therefore, to be at the mercy of world forces working out, or trying to work out some uniform equilibrium according to the ideal principles of laissez-faire capitalism'.[19] - i.e. no race to the bottom.

Broadly speaking, Keynes's view about what the structure of the British economy ought to be prevailed in the period 1945 to 1970. Britain was a mainly manufacturing economy: the share of manufacturing in national output and exports changed little from the 1920s to the 1970s. Until the 1970s, manufacturing represented just over 30 per cent of output, and around two thirds of British exports. Agriculture was subsidised. Finance – or the City of London – was – in the jargon – 'repressed' both by banking regulation and by capital controls. As one can see in retrospect, the economy, while growing steadily, also grew more and more inefficient, and less and less competitive. The litmus test was Britain's relatively slow rate of growth compared to its main rivals. Allied with this was a higher rate of inflation, the failure of 'industrial policy' to 'pick winners', the shambles of industrial relations. By the Thatcher time, the ideology of the free market had swept all before it. The structure of the economy should be left to the market, not to the government. The consumer, including the international consumer, should determine what was produced in the UK.

The last gasp of the older view was the House of Lords Select Committee Report on Overseas Trade in 1985. The context of its enquiry was the accelerated decline in British manufacturing. By the 1980s, the surpluses on trade in manufactured goods had turned into deficits. Manufacturing was now only one-fifth of the economy but still produced 40 per cent of export earnings. What would happen to our balance of trade when the surpluses from North Sea Oil ran out? The Report argued that we needed a favourable manufacturing balance to

19   JMK, CW, xxi, 238, 240-1

pay our way and prevent a decline in our living standards. Nicholas Kaldor said the Report had assembled the facts to 'demonstrate the inevitability of an economic crisis of catastrophic proportions', unless government took active steps to revive manufacturing industry. He cited the difference between the British and the French, German, and Japanese attitudes to manufacturing. The Chancellor Nigel Lawson dismissed the report as 'special pleading dressed up as analysis'. No one sector was more meritorious, and thus worthy of support, than another. Services would take up the slack of shrinking employment in manufacturing. And short-run current account deficits could always be financed.

Kaldor's catastrophe has not come to pass, despite the further shrinkage of manufacturing from 25 per cent to 10 per cent of GDP. But neither has the economy's performance been nearly as good as it was in the twenty five years after the war. Particularly important is the widening trade deficit, which Kaldor predicted in the 1980s. Services have not compensated for manufactures in our trade balance: the current account deficit is still 2.5 per cent of GDP after a 21 per cent depreciation of sterling.

I would like to make the case for rebalancing the economy on slightly different grounds from the earlier champions of manufacturing: to wit, the effect that different structures of the economy have on a government's revenue base.

Imagine an extreme case in which an economy pays for its food imports with its oil exports. The economy exports only oil and imports everything else it needs. Now, for some reason, its oil exports a shrink to zero – say, because of a blockade. It cannot therefore pay for the import of any of its necessaries. Before it can start producing more of its own food, a sizeable fraction of the population starves to death. The oil famine has produced a food famine.

This, as I said, is an extreme case, but it does draw attention to the strong conditions needed to realise the predicted gains from specialization. Security of supply is a key requirement. Globalization has been carried out on the assumption that this has ceased to be an issue: arguments for maintaining 'strategic' industries within one's national borders have faded away in all except the largest military powers.

However, there is another aspect of security which has received less attention: security of price. To go back to our previous example of the mono oil producer: almost the same consequences for the population would ensue if the oil price collapsed. The prices of goods traded on markets do not, in general, experience such extreme, life-endangering, swings. Nevertheless, the prices of commodities are much more volatile than those of manufactured goods and services, because they are much more influenced by climatic conditions, speculation, and so on. Look at the gyrations of the oil price in the last three years. Because of this factor, commodity producers are more vulnerable to 'shocks' than non-commodity producers. Hence the pressure in such countries to diversify away from commodities and/or to develop effective hedging systems against price swings.

This brings me to my main proposition. A country which is heavily dependent, as is Britain, on its financial sector, is in some respects in the position of a commodity producer. The reason is that the financial sector is inherently volatile. The securities traded on financial markets are subject to large short-term price fluctuations, because future prices are uncertain, and hedging is very costly. The financial sector is particularly prone to boom and bust.

Financial volatility affects all incomes, including the income of the government. Imagine you are living off the income of capital, and the value of your capital falls by half: your income is halved. This, in much less extreme form, is what happened to the British government after 2008. Because of its disproportionate reliance on inflated taxes from the financial sector, its revenues collapsed disproportionately when the financial sector failed. In 2007, the financial services sector was 8 per cent of the economy but contributed 14 per cent of the government's tax revenue. Today it is 10 per cent of the economy but contributes 11 per cent of the tax revenue. In figures, revenue from financial services has fallen over 20 per cent, from £68bn to £53bn. This disproportionate collapse in taxable profits of the financial services industry helps to explain why the British government's 'structural deficit' was much greater than those of countries with more balanced economies. It had become over-reliant on a particularly volatile revenue stream.

Assets are entitlements to income streams. That is why the individual investor is normally advised by his stockbroker to hold a diversified portfolio. If one asset loses its income-producing capacity, he will still be able to rely on the others.

I would like to suggest that a government, or state, is in a similar position. Given its macroeconomic and social responsibilities no government can (or should) remain indifferent to the distribution and performance of a nation's assets, human or physical, because on that depends its ability to fulfil its functions. Indifference would be justified only if all the assets had the same risk profile. But this is not true. Nor can the government rely on the tax system to equalise returns on the margin; the tax system is far too blunt to do this. The best that the government can do is to invest in a balanced portfolio, which is to say, to have a balanced economy.

How is this to be done? I have suggested the mechanism of a National Investment Bank. There are two arguments for such a Bank: a short term one and a structural one. In the context of the battle against the cuts, I have concentrated on the short-term argument: given the commitment to fiscal austerity, one needs such an institution to offset the depressive effects on investment of increased public sector saving. But there is also a well-known structural argument.

Private lending has always had its blind spots, those bits of the economy where productive enterprises have always struggled to raise capital. One example is SMEs – small and medium enterprises – which fall into what used to be called the "Macmillan gap". But in areas like infrastructure, the market failure is systemic.

Adam Smith gave the state "the duty of erecting and maintaining certain public works and certain public institutions which it can never be for the interest of any individuals or small numbers of individuals to erect and maintain, because the profit would never repay the expenses…though it may frequently do much more than repay it to a great society."[20] Smith identified roads, bridges, canals and harbours as public goods, and recommended that they be made self-financing by user charges. Smith also wanted the state to subsidise education.

What Smith was pointing out was that the social benefit of building a bridge or electrifying a railway is likely to be higher than the private return expected by an investor. As a result, infrastructure projects fail to attract the optimum amount of private capital. The high initial costs and long time horizons involved in infrastructure investment increase the risks to private profits. This makes infrastructure less attractive to the private investor than shorter term projects, even though those projects may not offer society such a high rate of return. Private money goes elsewhere, the bridge is never built, and society loses out. A National Investment Bank could bring public benefits back into investment decisions, financing the projects which make the most difference to the wider economy.

More than that, it could itself be a vehicle for rebalancing the economy. The biggest source of new growth may well be green technology, which has all the features which make private capital markets wary; it has long lead times, volume is critical to profitability, and it needs effective regulation. If the wider economic benefits aren't taken into account, Britain could miss its chance to profit from the new wave of sustainable technology. The government has already recognised the need for state-led investment with the Green Bank, but the Treasury has crippled it before it can even begin lending. A National Investment

20   Smith, *The Wealth of Nations*, pp. 687-88

Bank would take the longer view, channelling investment into the areas which promise future economic growth.

The Chinese Prime Minister is in town today to sign trade agreements with UK companies. Their strategy is a good example of the foresighted thinking a National Investment Bank would promote. China invests heavily in the development of green technology, even in companies, like Britain's, which compete against its state enterprises. This is because the Chinese government knows that the economic benefit won't be confined to the developer. Ultimately the technology will end up on assembly lines back in China, and deliver profits to the state. Can we afford not to have a strategy for investment?

25. Coordination versus Disintegration
New Statesman | October 10, 2011

Since its collapse in the autumn of 2008, the world economy has gone through three phases: a year or more of rapid decline; a bounce back in 2009-2010, which nevertheless did not amount to a full recovery; and a second, though so far much shallower, downturn this year.

The resulting damage over the past four years has been huge. The world economy contracted by 6 per cent between 2007 and 2009, and recovered 4 per cent. It is 10 per cent poorer than it would have been, had growth continued at the rate of 2007, and the pain is not yet over. Today, we are in the first stages of a second banking crisis. It may already be too late to avoid a "double dip", but it may still be possible to avoid a triple dip. For this we need a robust intellectual analysis of what is required to ensure durable recovery, and the collective political will to implement it.

Backdrop to the crisis

Economics is in a mess. With the shattering of the dominant Chicago School paradigm, whose rational expectations hypothesis ruled out, by assumption, the kind of collapse we have just experienced, two old masters, Friedrich von Hayek and John Maynard Keynes, have risen from the dead to renew the battles of the 1930s, equipped this time with explanations for what has gone wrong. We can label these "money glut" and "saving glut".

The Hayekian argument for the slump is that lax monetary policy made it possible for the commercial banks to lend more money to businesses than the public wanted to save out of its current income. Hence, a whole tranche of investments – "malinvestments", Hayek called them – was being financed by credit creation, not genuine saving. This led to a bubble in the real estate and financial sectors which powered a consumption boom. When (belatedly) the money tap was turned off, the bubble burst and the American economy slumped. The slump is simply the liquidation of the unsound investments.

By contrast, the problem for Keynesians was not insufficient saving, but insufficient investment. Investment is governed by uncertainty, while saving is a stable fraction of income. Keynes's economy tips over into recession when, for some reason, profit expectations decline relative to the volume of saving being done. Businesses start to prefer liquidity to investment. This pushes up the rate of interest, or cost of borrowing, just when you want it to come down. Saving and investment are then brought back into balance, not by a fall in interest rates, but by a fall in incomes. The recession of 2008-2009 was caused by a collapse in investment, not by overindebtedness; overindebtedness was a consequence, not a cause.

Both explanations have an international dimension. The Hayekian story starts with the over-issuing of dollars by the US Federal Reserve, made possible by the dollar's role as the world's leading reserve currency. This enabled Americans to live beyond their means and to spend more than they produced.

The Keynesian story starts with Chinese over-saving. The Chinese save a much higher proportion of their incomes than their economy, as organised, can absorb. It was the voluntary recycling of excess Chinese savings into the US economy by means of the Chinese central bank's purchase of US Treasury bills which allowed the United States to become the world's "consumer of last resort". The "money glut" in the US was a consequence, not a cause, of the more fundamental "saving glut" in China.

The two stories are derived from contrasting theories about how a market economy works. The first sees it as a self-regulating mechanism, in which the "invisible hand" smoothly channels the self-interested actions of individuals towards a social optimum in the absence of monetary disturbances. The Keynesians accept the social value of the market system, but deny that, in the presence of irreducible uncertainty, it is optimally self-regulating. The "invisible" hand guides economies not to a social optimum but to "underemployment equilibrium". As such, government intervention is needed to ensure full use of potential resources.

On a cool view, there are elements of truth in both explanations of the recession. We do not have to choose between American profligacy and Chinese frugality. Our policies for recovery have to deal with both contributions to the unravelling of prosperity.

Austerity v stimulus

The differences just described over the origin of the crisis underpin the present debate between austerity and stimulus. According to Meghnad Desai, writing in the *Financial Times* of 15 September, "The long recession is a Hayekian phenomenon and not a Keynesian one ... The need is to deleverage, not to spend." The private and public sectors alike need to increase their saving, even though this will reduce aggregate demand in the short run. Letting assets find their proper value will bring genuine demand at realistic prices and punish those who have taken wrong decisions.

There will be more pain in the short term, but the Keynesian alternative of stimulus delays the adjustment, unfairly forcing taxpayers to pay the price of rescuing those who took too much risk. The boom was the illusion; the slump is the opportunity to liquidate the malinvestments.

To this, Keynesians pose two objections. First, they deny that there was "too much" spending in the US economy before the collapse. There were no signs of general overheating: inflation was low, and there was no shortage of labour. What they would concede to the Hayekians is that cheap money made possible a great deal of misdirected, or speculative investment, which fuelled a wealth-driven consumption boom. But this is not the same as saying that there was overinvestment in the strict sense that further investment would have yielded a zero rate of return, or that there was too much consumption in general. It is absurd to believe that the demand for goods and services of those 46 million Americans living below the poverty line had reached the point of saturation. The houses and construction facilities built in the bubble economy are still there: they require an increase, not a reduction, in the incomes of the low-paid in order to become "affordable".

But more fundamentally, Keynesians argue that, even if the Hayekian diagnosis is right, the remedy of austerity is wrong. It derives, they say, from the medieval medical practice of bleeding a sick person to purge the rottenness from his blood – a species of cure that frequently led to the death of the patient. Lionel Robbins, retracting his opposition to Keynesian stimulus policies in the 1930s, wrote:

> "Assuming that the original diagnosis of excessive financial ease and mistaken real investment was correct – which is certainly not a settled matter – to treat what developed subsequently [by austerity policies] was as unsuitable as denying blankets and stimulants to a drunk who has fallen into an icy pond on the ground that his original trouble was overheating".[21]

(Compare this with the German finance minister, Wolfgang Schäuble: "You can't cure an alcoholic by giving him alcohol.") The point is this: if both the government and the private sector are trying to increase their saving at the same time, you don't just liquidate the bad investments, you kill the economy as well, by reducing national income until everyone is too poor to save.

That is why I have been arguing in the UK that when private enterprise is asleep, for lack of effective demand, the state must step in to stimulate the moribund investment machine back into lively activity.

The truth is that the policy of all-round "cutting down" increases the problem of indebtedness. The bond markets have diagnosed

21   Robbins, *Autobiography of an Economist*, p. 154

accurately that, in the absence of growth policies, one lot of debts after another will become "unsustainable". Both the national debt and the debts of private institutions will shrink automatically as a fraction of national income if national income grows, and conversely will grow if it shrinks. Growth, not debt reduction, should be the chief aim of economic policy today. Where there are too many debt collectors, they end up ruining themselves. The eurozone today is awful witness to this truth.

The Global Economy in Crisis

With austerity in the ascendant, the world recovery is petering out. Europe is on the edge of a precipice, in a feedback loop from bank insolvency to an explosion of sovereign debt to a second round of bank insolvency. The United States is in little better shape, with its fiscal policy paralysed and the markets expecting a Japanese-style stagnation.

Latin America, the Middle East and Russia are benefiting from a commodity boom. Of their main markets, however, the US and Europe are hardly growing, and China is slowing down as Beijing tries to rein in an inflationary bubble in real estate, and because its export-led growth depends on the continuing increase in American and European demand. If China's voracious appetite for commodities slows, growth in Latin America, the Middle East and Russia will grind to a halt, which in turn will limit demand from them for Chinese goods. So the circle of pain widens, as each misfortune feeds back on itself.

The plain fact is that there is too little aggregate demand in the world, and the net effect of all the policies being pursued is to reduce it further. So, what will the future bring?

We know what happened in the 1930s: the world economy broke up. The conventional wisdom is that this is impossible today under any circumstances. The cliché has it that economic integration is irreversible; that the revolution in information and communications is ineluctably turning the world into a "global village". However, this benign prospect ignores the possibility of great crises and collapses. People were saying exactly the same thing in 1914. Historically, globalisation has come in waves, which recede under the impact of crisis and catastrophe as economic life retreats to the relatively safe haven of national jurisdictions.

We have reached the end of that phase of globalisation in which we dealt with the problem of permanently mispriced currencies by means of recycling mechanisms that pumped up speculative bubbles. But what follows it? There are two alternative hypotheses, which may be described as Disintegration and Co-ordination.

Disintegration versus Coordination

The first hypothesis is that, as we fail to solve our problems globally, the global economy will start to fragment. At present, domestic demand is being suppressed both by countries that depend heavily on export-led growth and by countries that are trying to reduce their current account deficits. What this signals is that the global authorities are engaged in a simultaneous effort, for different reasons, to reduce aggregate demand.

This is completely the wrong policy. Christine Lagarde, the new managing director of the International Monetary Fund, is right to argue that fiscal retrenchment in the teeth of a recession is suicide. The break will come when the deficit countries, unable to endure any further "bleeding", start to resort to currency depreciation and protectionism. If the eurozone fails to organise growth policies, Greece and possibly other eurozone countries will resume their monetary and trade independence. Currency and trade wars will erupt across the globe: indeed, these wars have already begun.

The second hypothesis, Co-ordination, is what Gordon Brown calls a "G20 growth compact". Essentially, he is calling for a revival of the spirit of international co-operation which produced the stimulus of 2009 and halted the slide into another Great Depression.

Elements of such a compact would include a reform of the global monetary system, aiming to end the era of current account imbalances; a reform of the financial system, aiming to avoid the excesses of bank lending that triggered the crisis; and macroeconomic policies that aim to boost world demand in the short run.

Progress has come on the second item. Basel III has accepted the need for the banks to hold more capital against their liabilities. Individual countries have also begun to beef up their regulatory systems. In the UK, the Vickers report has proposed splitting the retail from the investment functions of banks. Hayek would have approved.

The more fundamental problem is the political power of the big banks. Not only does finance have to be reformed, it must be tamed. Winston Churchill put it well in 1925, as chancellor of the exchequer: "I would rather see finance less proud and industry more content." So far no government has had the guts to stand up to the banks. This suggests that financial re-regulation will be emasculated.

On the other two items, there is no progress to report at all. Reform of the world monetary system needs be based on a grand bargain, mainly between China and the US, on reserves and exchange rates, but there is no sign yet of any serious attempt to achieve this. As for the third item, the only macroeconomic co-ordination is in the direction of cutting down, not building up, the world economy. There is no investment in growth.

Yet the world economy cannot cut its way out of recession: it has to grow its way out. If the bond markets force deficit reduction programmes on highly indebted governments, states must look to alternative instruments – such as national or regional investment banks – to mobilise private savings going to waste for want of profitable investment opportunities.

Sovereign wealth funds and pension funds would invest in growth if there was any growth going on. As it is, they invest in government debt, which carries low yields but is at least relatively safe. The former US deputy Treasury secretary Roger Altman has made the point that historically low yields on long-term government debt in the US, the UK and Germany can be explained only by anticipation of "negligible demand for capital".

Of the two scenarios, Disintegration is the more likely. This is not just because political leadership is not up to the job of forging a global compact, but because the adjustments required of our current national economic models are too great to be undertaken voluntarily. Americans will need to consume less and export more; China and Germany will have to consume more and export less. Such change requires a fundamental rethinking of ways of living into which all three countries are locked.

In the US case, adjustment will require a break with a credit-fuelled economy, which is the only way American capitalism has of dealing with the vast inequalities of wealth and income that it has created by outsourcing most of its manufacturing to low-wage countries. There is little sign, however, of the US being willing to rethink its version of capitalism.

In the case of the Chinese, their country's low consumption ratio, as Michael Pettis, on his blog *China Financial Markets*, points out, is "fundamental to the [Chinese] growth model, and the suppression of consumption is a consequence of the very policies – low wage growth relative to productivity growth, an undervalued currency and, above all, artificially low interest rates – that have generated the furious GDP growth".

Germany, too, is locked in to export-led growth, and does not seem fully to understand that if it beggars its European neighbours by running a permanent export surplus, it will end up by beggaring itself.

If China and Germany insist on being 21st-century mercantilists – exporting more than they import – the rest of the world will start to protect itself against them. Germany's policy will lead to the breakdown of the eurozone, China's to the breakdown of the world trading and payments system.

The two scenarios – Co-ordination and Disintegration – have in common that they presuppose more reliance by countries or groups of countries on domestic sources of growth, and less on foreign trade. That is what we mean when we talk of a more balanced world economy. The sole question is whether the retreat from the wilder shores of globalisation will be orderly or disorderly: whether we drift into the bloc economics of the 1930s, or whether we have the wisdom to build a managed and modified form of globalisation, free from the illusion that everything can be left safely to the markets.

And here's the point – a disorderly, acrimonious retreat from globalisation is bound to overshoot the mark, reviving the economics and the politics of the 1930s; but leading, in an era of nuclear proliferation, to consequences that are even more terrifying. So we must resolutely work for the best, without illusion, and with only modest hope.

VI. THE CRISIS CONTINUES

The first edition ended in 2011 with the British economy sliding towards a double-dip recession. It continued to 'flat-line' throughout 2012. The recovery started in the first quarter of 2013 and has continued for three quarters.

26. Does Debt Matter?

Project Syndicate I January 20, 2012

Europe is now haunted by the spectre of debt. All European leaders quail before it. To exorcise the demon, they are putting their economies through the wringer.

It doesn't seem to be helping. Their economies are still tumbling, and the debt continues to grow. The credit ratings agency Standard & Poor's has just downgraded the sovereign-debt ratings of nine eurozone countries, including France. The United Kingdom is likely to follow.

To anyone not blinded by folly, the explanation for this mass downgrade is obvious. If you deliberately aim to shrink your GDP, your debt-to-GDP ratio is bound to grow. The only way to cut your debt (other than by default) is to get your economy to grow.

Fear of debt is rooted in human nature; so the extinction of it as a policy aim seems right to the average citizen. Everyone knows what financial debt means: money owed, often borrowed. To be in debt can produce anxiety if one is uncertain whether, when the time comes, one will be able to repay what one owes.

This anxiety is readily transferred to national debt – the debt owed by a government to its creditors. How, people ask, will governments repay all of the hundreds of billions of dollars that they owe? As British Prime Minister David Cameron put it: "Government debt is the same as credit-card debt; it's got to be paid back."

The next step readily follows: in order to repay, or at least reduce, the national debt, the government must eliminate its budget deficit, because the excess of spending over revenue continually adds to the national debt. Indeed, if the government fails to act, the national debt will become, in today's jargon, "unsustainable."

Again, an analogy with household debt readily suggests itself. My death does not extinguish my debt, reasons the sensible citizen. My creditors will have the first claim on my estate – everything that I wanted to leave to my children. Similarly, a debt left unpaid too long by a government is a burden on future generations: I may enjoy the benefits of government extravagance, but my children will have to foot the bill.

That is why deficit reduction is at the center of most governments' fiscal policy today. A government with a "credible" plan for "fiscal consolidation" supposedly is less likely to default on its debt, or leave it for the future to pay. This will, it is thought, enable the government to borrow money more cheaply than it would otherwise be able to do, in turn lowering interest rates for private borrowers, which should boost economic activity. So fiscal consolidation is the royal road to economic recovery.

This, the official doctrine of most developed countries today, contains at least five major fallacies, which pass largely unnoticed, because the narrative is so plausible.

First, governments, unlike private individuals, do not have to "repay" their debts. A government of a country with its own central bank and its own currency can simply continue to borrow by printing the money which is lent to it. This is not true of countries in the eurozone. But their governments do not have to repay their debts, either. If their (foreign) creditors put too much pressure on them, they simply default. Default is bad. But life after default goes on much as before.

Second, deliberately cutting the deficit is not the best way for a government to balance its books. Deficit reduction in a depressed economy is the road not to recovery, but to contraction, because it means cutting the national income on which the government's revenues depend. This will make it harder, not easier, for it to cut the deficit. The British government already must borrow £112 billion ($172 billion) more than it had planned when it announced its deficit-reduction plan in June 2010.

Third, the national debt is not a net burden on future generations. Even if it gives rise to future tax liabilities (and some of it will), these will be transfers from taxpayers to bond holders. This may have disagreeable distributional consequences. But trying to reduce it now will be a net burden on future generations: income will be lowered immediately, profits will fall, pension funds will be diminished, investment projects will be canceled or postponed, and houses, hospitals, and schools will not be built. Future generations will be worse off, having been deprived of assets that they might otherwise have had.

Fourth, there is no connection between the size of national debt and the price that a government must pay to finance it. The interest rates that Japan, the United States, the UK, and Germany pay on their national debt are equally low, despite vast differences in their debt levels and fiscal policies.

Finally, low borrowing costs for governments do not automatically reduce the cost of capital for the private sector. After all, corporate borrowers do not borrow at the "risk-free" yield of, say, US Treasury bonds, and evidence shows that monetary expansion can push down the interest rate on government debt, but have hardly any effect on new bank lending to firms or households. In fact, the causality is the reverse: the reason why government interest rates in the UK and elsewhere are so low is that interest rates for private-sector loans are so high.

As with "the specter of Communism" that haunted Europe in Karl Marx's famous manifesto, so today "[a]ll the powers of old Europe have entered into a holy alliance to exorcise" the specter of national debt. But statesmen who aim to liquidate the debt should recall another famous specter – the spectre of revolution.

27. Good and Bad Deficits

Project Syndicate | February 22, 2012

"Deficits are always bad," thunder fiscal hawks. Not so, replies strategic investment analyst H. Wood Brock in an interesting new book, The American Gridlock. A proper assessment, Brock argues, depends on the "composition and quality of total government spending."

Government deficits incurred on current spending for services or transfers are bad, because they produce no revenue and add to the national debt. Deficits resulting from capital spending, by contrast, are – or can be – good. If wisely administered, such spending produces a revenue stream that services and eventually extinguishes the debt; more importantly, it raises productivity, and thus improves a country's long-run growth potential.

From this distinction follows an important fiscal rule: governments' current spending should normally be balanced by taxation. To this extent, efforts nowadays to reduce deficits on current spending are justified, but only if they are fully replaced by capital-spending programs. Indeed, reducing current spending and increasing capital spending should be carried out in lock step.

Brock's argument is that, given the state of its economy, the United States cannot return to full employment on the basis of current policy. The recovery is too feeble, and the country needs to invest an additional $1 trillion annually for ten years on transport facilities and education. The government should establish a National Infrastructure Bank to provide the finance by borrowing directly, attracting private-sector funds, or a mixture of the two. (I have proposed a similar institution in the United Kingdom.)

The distinction between capital and current spending (and thus between "good" and "bad" deficits) is old hat to any student of public finance. But we forget knowledge at such an alarming rate that it is worth re-stating it, particularly with deficit hawks in power in the UK and Europe, though fortunately not (yet) in the US.

According to proposals agreed at an informal European Council meeting on January 30, all EU members are to amend their constitutions to introduce a balanced-budget rule that caps annual structural deficits at 0.5 per cent of GDP. This ceiling can be raised only in a deep depression or other exceptional circumstances, allowing for counter-cyclical policy so long as it is agreed that the additional deficit is cyclical, rather than structural. Otherwise, violations would automatically trigger fines of up to 0.1 per cent of GDP.

The UK is one of two EU countries (alongside the Czech Republic) that refused to sign this "fiscal compact," acceptance of which is required to gain access to European bailout funds. But Britain's government has the identical aim of reducing its current deficit of 10 per cent of GDP to near zero in five years.

An argument commonly heard in support of such policies is that the "bond vigilantes" will demand nothing less. And the finances of some European governments (and Latin American governments in the recent past) have been so parlous that this reaction is understandable.

But that is not true of the US or the UK, which both have large fiscal deficits. And most countries were adhering to reasonably tight fiscal discipline before the crisis of 2008 undermined their banks, cut their tax revenues, and forced up their sovereign debt.

At the same time, we should not attribute current enthusiasm for fiscal retrenchment to such contingencies. At its heart lies the belief that all government spending above a necessary minimum is wasteful. Europe has its own Tea Party crackpots who loathe the welfare state and want it abolished or radically pared, and who are convinced that all state-sponsored capital spending is a "boondoggle" – just so many roads, bridges, and railway lines to nowhere that soak up their money in corruption and inefficiency.

Those who believe this are unfazed by the corruption and waste that characterizes much private-sector spending. And they prefer the total waste of letting millions of people sit idle (Brock reckons that 16 per cent of the American workforce is unemployed, underemployed, or too discouraged to seek work) to the possibly partial waste of programs that put them to work, nurture their skills, and equip the country with assets.

One can criticize details of Brock's case: a deeper understanding of Keynes would have given him a more persuasive response to the objection that, if state-financed projects were worth doing, the private sector would be doing them. Before long, we will have to provide answers to these questions, because the pre-slump fiscal rules that the Europeans are vainly trying to strengthen were not up to the job.

We are far from having worked out a post-recession theory of macroeconomic policy, but certain elements are clear. In the future, fiscal and monetary policy will have to work together: neither on its own can stabilize inherently unstable market economies. Monetary policy will have to do much more than it did before 2008 to restrain financial markets' "irrational exuberance." And we need a new, unambiguous system of fiscal accounting that distinguishes between tax-funded government spending and public spending that pays for itself.

Above all, we need to recognize that the state's role goes beyond maintaining external security and domestic law and order. As Adam Smith wrote in The Wealth of Nations:

"The third and last duty of the sovereign....is that of erecting and maintaining those public institutions and those public works, which though they may be in the highest degree advantageous to a great society, are, however, of such a nature, that the profit could never repay the expense to any individual, or small number of individuals; and which it, therefore, cannot be expected that any individual, or small number of individuals, should erect or maintain."

Chief among these public works, for Smith, are those that "facilitate the commerce of any country, such as good roads, bridges, navigable canals, harbors, etc." Another piece of forgotten knowledge that Smith also mentions is the importance of education. He is right to do so, however much today's deficit hawks seem, by their behavior, to prove the opposite.

28. George Osborne is wrong. Austerity is for the boom years, not the slump

The Guardian | March 23, 2012

The main test of a budget at this time is what it does for the recovery and growth of the British economy. George Osborne has repeatedly made clear that he wants to be judged by this test. He believes that deficit reduction is a growth policy which will be vindicated by its results. Growth has been postponed but, he insists, it is about to happen. So is he right?

Some people believe this debate is not even worth having. For instance, the economist Tim Congdon has dismissed the debate between austerity and growth as "nonsense". The evidence, he claimed, was clear: countries with smaller government deficits grow faster than countries with larger ones. This is untrue, as a general rule. According to the International Monetary Fund, the US, whose government debt to GDP ratio is 105 per cent and whose deficit is 7.9 per cent of GDP, is projected to grow by 1.8 per cent this year; while Britain, with a debt ratio of 81 per cent and a deficit of 7.0 per cent of GDP, is expected to grow by just 0.8 per cent.

Intuitively one would expect economic growth to shrink the deficit and stagnation to enlarge it, because growth increases government revenues and reduces expenditure on the unemployed. The fact that net public sector borrowing in February was £15.2bn, up from £8.9bn last February and almost double the forecast £8bn, confirms this expectation.

Osborne claims his deficit reduction plan is on course and borrowing has come in below targets – but these are the same targets that were revised upwards by £112bn only in November. Keynes's remark, "look after unemployment and the budget will look after itself" is more to the point than Osborne's "look after the budget and unemployment will look after itself".

Osborne's claim rests on the view that a shrinking deficit will automatically, if mysteriously, revive the "animal spirits" of businessmen, while confidence in the government's finances will reduce the cost of its borrowing. However, the opposite logic is more compelling. If the government is cutting its own spending at the same time as households and businesses are cutting theirs, the result is a fall in total spending which means a fall in total buying. This depresses output and employment. And the low cost of government borrowing may not be a sign of confidence at all. It may mean the money has nowhere better to go, or simply that the Bank of England is busily buying up government debt.

Osborne has said the government cannot afford to spend at the present rate because it hasn't got the money. But if the country were more fully employed, the government would receive extra revenue – which would make its spending "affordable".

Osborne aims to cut down waste in the public services. And there is a lot of waste. But cutting waste also means cutting jobs, and that creates even greater waste. It is odd that people who pride themselves on sound thinking prefer the total waste of unemployment to the partial waste of public employment. The most extravagant housing scheme still leaves the nation with houses. Unemployment leaves it with worse than nothing, for prolonged idleness renders the unemployed unemployable.

Ed Miliband was right to highlight the failure of Osborne's "budget for growth" last year. Twelve months ago the forecast growth for 2012 was three times the meagre 0.8 per cent figure revealed by the Office for Budget Responsibility, now hailed by Osborne as an improvement. He blames the eurozone crisis and high oil prices for the continued sluggishness of the recovery – anything but his own policy. Labour has also started to argue that austerity is not enough: hence Miliband's welcome endorsement of the idea of a British investment bank, which could become a powerful engine for jolting us out of our semi-slump.

But Labour has not engaged directly with Osborne's claim that budgetary austerity is necessary to get us out of our economic hole. Indeed, it would be difficult for it to do so, since the logic was accepted by Osborne's predecessor, Alistair Darling. Instead the party has skirmished at the edges – about the speed of the cuts and distribution of sacrifice. So it has been bereft of the strongest anti-cuts argument: the boom, not the slump, is the time for Treasury austerity.

The debate we need to have is intellectual, not party political. One doesn't have to be a Conservative to support Osborne's cuts (evidently the Lib Dems do), and one doesn't have to be Labour to oppose them. The intellectual debate opens up a wide field for distinguishing between good and bad capitalism. It needs to be framed in a European as well as a British framework, since the eurozone's recovery prospects are even more dire than our own, and Europe offers examples of a more benign capitalism than our own Anglo-American model. It is only through vigorous intellectual give and take that one can hope to rekindle people's interest in politics.

29. Down with Debt Weight
Project Syndicate | April 18, 2012

Nearly four years after the start of the global financial crisis, many are wondering why economic recovery is taking so long. Indeed, its sluggishness has confounded even the experts. According to the International Monetary Fund, the world economy should have grown by 4.4 per cent in 2011, and should grow by 4.5 per cent in 2012. In fact, the latest figures from the World Bank indicate that growth reached just 2.7 per cent in 2011, and will slow this year to 2.5 per cent – a figure that may well need to be revised downwards.

There are two possible reasons for the discrepancy between forecast and outcome. Either the damage caused by the financial crisis was more serious than people realized, or the economic medicine prescribed was less efficacious than policymakers believed.

In fact, the gravity of the banking crisis was quickly grasped. Huge stimulus packages were implemented in 2008-9, led by the United States and China, coordinated by Britain, and with the reluctant support of Germany. Interest rates were slashed, insolvent banks were bailed out, the printing presses were turned on, taxes were cut, and public spending was boosted. Some countries devalued their currencies.

As a result, the slide was halted, and the rebound was faster than forecasters expected. But the stimulus measures transformed a banking crisis into a fiscal and sovereign-debt crisis. From 2010 onwards, governments started to raise taxes and cut spending in response to growing fears of sovereign default. At that point, the recovery went into reverse.

As Carmen Reinhart and Kenneth Rogoff tell it in their masterly book *This Time is Different*, there is no secure way of short-circuiting a deep banking crisis. The crisis originates with "excessive debt accumulation," which makes economies "vulnerable to crises of confidence." Commercial banks have to be bailed out by governments; then governments have to be bailed out by commercial banks. In the end, both have to be bailed out by central banks.

All of this, according to Reinhart and Rogoff, involves a "protracted and pronounced contraction in economic activity." They reckon that the average length of post-war crises has been 4.4 years – the time it takes for the necessary "de-leveraging" to occur – after which the crisis of confidence is over and economic growth revives.

However, there is something missing in the story. Recovery from the Great Depression took about 10 years, more than twice the post-war average. Reinhart and Rogoff offer a couple of reasons for the difference in recovery rates: the slow policy response to the Great Depression and the gold standard, which meant that individual countries could not export their way out of depression. In other words, fiscal policy and the monetary-policy regime have a decisive influence both on the depth of the collapse and how long before the economy recovers.

It is also significant that big financial collapses occurred again in the 1970s, after being virtually absent in the 1950s and 1960s, when the Keynesian system of managed economies and the Bretton Woods system of managed exchange rates was in place. The major post-war crises that Reinhart and Rogoff consider run from 1977 to 2001. They occurred because regulation of banks and controls on capital movements were lifted; they were shorter than in the 1930s because the policy responses were not idiotic.

Indonesian president Susilo Bambang Yudhoyono emphasized that point earlier this month, boasting to British Prime Minister David Cameron that Indonesia's successful recovery plan after the 1998 collapse was inspired by John Maynard Keynes. "We must ensure that the people can buy; we must ensure that industries can produce..."

Today, many governments, especially in the eurozone, seem to have run out of policy options. With fiscal austerity all the rage, they have given up ensuring that "people can buy" and "industries can produce." Central banks have been handed the job of keeping economies afloat, but most of the money that they print remains stuck in the banking system, unable to arrest stagnating consumption and falling investment.

Moreover, the eurozone itself is a mini-gold standard, with heavily indebted members unable to devalue their currencies, because they have no currencies to devalue. So, given that Chinese growth, too, is slowing, the world economy seems destined to crawl along the bottom for some time yet, with unemployment rising in some countries to 20 per cent or more.

With fiscal, monetary, and exchange-rate policies blocked, is there a way out of prolonged recession? John Geanakoplos of Yale University has been arguing for big debt write-offs. Rather than waiting to get rid of debt through bankruptcies, governments should "mandate debt forgiveness." They could buy bad loans from lenders and forgive part of the principal payable by borrowers, simultaneously reducing lenders' collateral requirements and borrowers' debt overhang. In the US, the Term Asset-Backed Securities Loan Facility (TALF) program and the Public-Private Investment Program (PPIP) were in effect debt-forgiveness schemes aimed at sub-prime mortgage holders, but on too small a scale.

But the principle of debt forgiveness clearly has applications for public debt as well, especially in the eurozone. Those who fear excessive public debt are the banks that hold it. Junk public bonds are no safer for them than junk private bonds. Both lenders and borrowers would be better off from a comprehensive debt cancelation. So would citizens whose livelihoods are being destroyed by governments' desperate attempts to de-leverage.

Philosophically, the debt-forgiveness approach rests on the belief that creditors share culpability for defaults with debtors, since they made the bad loans in the first place. As long as the borrower has not misled the lender at the time of taking the loan, the lender bears at least some responsibility for the transaction.

In 1918, Keynes urged the cancelation of inter-Allied debts arising from World War I. "We shall never be able to move again, unless we can free our limbs from these paper shackles," he wrote. And, in 1923, his call became a warning that today's policymakers would do well to heed: "The absolutists of contract…are the real parents of revolution."

30. Nick Clegg's U-turn for the better
The Guardian I May 25, 2012

The deputy prime minister, Nick Clegg, has promised a "massive amplification" of state-backed investments in housing and infrastructure. Words only. But if the words mean anything, they amount to a huge U-turn – a belated acknowledgment that austerity has not brought recovery.

The realisation that austerity is having a dampening effect on economic activity has spread throughout Europe. Everyone has started to talk about policies for growth. This is a marked shift from the previous story which asserted that public austerity was the growth policy – that workers sacked from the bloated public sector would soon find employment in the more productive private sector. But no one in power has admitted that the previous story was wrong.

Instead the U-turn is disguised by claiming that it was only austerity that has given the British government the "credibility" to switch course. As Clegg put it, it is only because the markets "no longer have their foot on our throats" that the government can "use its balance sheet" to help revive private sector investment. This is discreditable nonsense. But it has an air of plausibility.

It is true that the government's deficit has fallen from 11 per cent of GDP to 8.3 per cent in the past two years. This may be counted as a minor success for the deficit reduction policy – though much less than the government promised. Most of it was achieved by cutting capital spending – the very spending Clegg promises to revive. Had this spending not been cut, the deficit would now be smaller, because the economy would be larger. Austerity has caused the economy to shrink, not grow.

It is not true, as Clegg claims, that the government faced a debt emergency when it came to office. Yes, it can now borrow at a couple of percentage points below the last government. But the Labour government's borrowing rate was already at its lowest for 10 years. To claim that but for George Osborne's austerity programme the cost of our government debt would have shot up to the Greek rate was sheer scare-mongering.

In any case, the reason why the British government can sell its bonds so cheaply today has much less to do with "confidence' induced by fiscal austerity than with Britain having a central bank licenced to print money, and with austerity having depressed other investment prospects so much that gilts remain the only place to park cash. Cheap money for the government is the sign of a sick, not healthy, economy.

The truth is that the chancellor could have avoided most of the deficit reduction pain and achieved a better deficit outcome had he started by making the critical distinction between current and capital spending. Instead of pledging to eliminate the whole deficit by the end of this parliament, he should have asserted that it was legitimate for the government to go on borrowing for capital spending. The reason is that government debt issued to finance a capital account deficit is not a claim on future tax revenues, since it adds to those revenues, both directly and indirectly. It is what every company does when it borrows to invest.

Osborne should also have said that in a slump it is especially necessary to keep government-backed capital spending going, as it is the only thing that can offset the dampening effect on private demand of the slump itself, and of cuts in current spending which might be necessary to reassure the markets. But that would have required a chancellor less viscerally hostile to public spending than is George Osborne, and a Treasury less trapped by false economic theory.

In Britain and Europe, policymakers are moving from a state of denying that their policies are wrong to one of cognitive dissonance – holding two contradictory theories simultaneously. The two theories are austerity and prosperity. This is a welcome sign of progress. Above it towers the peak of coherence. Drop austerity, go for growth and the debt will start to come down.

31. The Austere Land

The New Republic | June 22, 2012

The last four years have created what economists call a "natural experiment" in economic policy. As a consequence of deregulation and globalization, Britain and the United States experienced the financial crisis of 2008 in much the same way. Large parts of the banking system collapsed and had to be rescued; the real economy went into a nosedive and had to be stimulated. But after 2010, the United States continued to stimulate its economy, while Britain chose the stonier path of austerity.

The British are no more wedded to the idea of fiscal austerity than are the Americans. The Victorian aim of an annual budgetary surplus (in order to allow for the repayment of debt) has long since vanished. Both countries experienced only occasional surpluses in the postwar years associated with exceptional booms. The divergence of the two countries lies not in underlying attitudes but in political and institutional circumstances.

First, the British entered the crisis with a largely discredited Labour government; the Americans with a largely discredited Republican administration. The political swing gave power to the traditional spenders in the United States and the traditional budget-cutters in Britain. Second, despite their small-government rhetoric, Republicans have actually always accepted, and indeed promoted, large deficits in the name of national security. Third, whereas the U.S. Treasury is simply an agency of government, the British Treasury has always assumed that it should control, not facilitate, government spending. Finally, Britain, with European examples in mind, was concerned that foreign bondholders would take fright at the growth of the national debt—at least, this became the grand rationalization of austerity policy after the Greek crisis flared up in 2010.

These factors help explain the differing fortunes of John Maynard Keynes in the two countries. Homegrown in Britain, Keynesian policy was enthusiastically embraced by British governments immediately after the war. In the United States, full-blooded Keynesianism started only with John F. Kennedy and Lyndon Johnson in the 1960s. The United States under Ronald Reagan and Britain under Margaret Thatcher abandoned official Keynesianism in the 1980s, but the taxcutting, defense-boosting commitments of the Republican Party kept unofficial Keynesianism alive in the United States long after it had been relinquished in Keynes's own country. When George W. Bush, in announcing his stimulus measures of 2001, declared that budget deficits were justified by war, a recession, or a national emergency, Milton Friedman deplored the fact that "crude Keynesianism has risen from the dead." Paradoxically, Keynesianism, unacknowledged and often reviled, chimed in with some constants in U.S. political life better than it did in Britain, where it is still customary to pay homage to the master while ignoring his teaching.

So what does the experiment in economic policy tell us? At the start of the crisis, leading economic indicators in the United States and Britain were broadly similar: a government deficit of around 2.7 per cent of gross domestic product (GDP), inflation of around 2.5 per cent, and unemployment around 5 per cent. The greatest differences were in GDP growth, with Britain growing at 3.5 per cent in 2007 and the United States at 1.9 per cent, and in the debt-to-GDP ratio, with Britain at 38 per cent and the United States at 48 per cent. In the autumn of 2008, both countries saw their financial and real economies rapidly contract. By the third quarter 2009, GDP had fallen by 5 per cent in the United States and 5.9 per cent in Britain, with unemployment rising sharply.

Both the Bush and Obama administrations and the British Labour Government subscribed to a Keynesian "savings-glut" interpretation of the crisis. According to this view, excessive saving in East Asia led to current account surpluses and created global deflationary pressure. Cheap money and expansionary fiscal policy in the West in the runup to the crisis were necessary responses. The resulting asset bubbles were not the fault of expansionary policy, but due to the fact that the money was channeled into speculation rather than investment. Once the bubble burst, savings rose and aggregate demand collapsed.

It followed that recovery required a boost to demand. As President Barack Obama put it: "It is expected that we are going to lose about a trillion dollars worth of [private] demand this year [and] a trillion dollars of demand next year because of the contraction in the economy. So the reason that this [stimulus package] has to be big is to try to fill some of that lost demand." Britain's Labour government agreed. In 2008–2009, Prime Minister Gordon Brown pumped an extra $41 billion into the British economy; in February of 2009, Obama signed into law a $787 billion fiscal stimulus package. Insolvent banks were bailed out and the central banks of both countries started "quantitative easing"—effectively, printing money—in an effort to expand the supply of credit by forcing down bank lending rates.

The activist policies had an immediate impact in both countries. A year after the onset of the crisis, GDP growth started to pick up. However, while stimulus measures prevented another Great Depression, they helped expand government debt. In 2007, both the British and U.S. government deficits were 2.7 per cent of GDP; in 2010, the figures were 9.9 per cent and 10.5 per cent, respectively.

Chicago economist Robert Lucas has ruefully remarked that "everyone is a Keynesian in a foxhole." But once stimulus policies removed the danger of prolonged depression, ideological conservatism reasserted itself. The fact that the bond markets started betting against highly indebted governments gave fiscal hawks an excuse to cut state spending under the guise of restoring "credibility" and "sustainability"; in Britain, these ostensible virtues became the basis of official policy after the general election of 2010. Britain's Conservative spin doctors fueled the debt aversion with images from the streets of Athens and analogies between the private and public purse. Unless the state learned to live within its means, Britain would become "another Greece." Austerity, not stimulus, was the road to recovery.

As austerity policies took hold in most of Europe, a Hayekian "money-glut" analysis of the origins of the slump replaced the Keynesian "savings-glut" one. According to Friedrich Hayek, slumps result from overly loose monetary policy. Excessive money-creation by the central bank makes it possible for banks to lend more than the public wants to save. Hayek called the creditfinanced investment that results from this "mal-investment." Malinvestment manifested itself mainly in rapidly rising housing and asset prices. These prices were unsustainable, because they were based on debt, not genuine saving. Once the default rates on mortgages went up, the banks found that their AAA rated assets had become junk. So they stopped lending.

The collapse of the financial economy led to a sharp contraction of the real economy. In this view of things, the main requirement for recovery was to increase saving and liquidate the malinvestments. Fiscal stimulus would only delay a genuine recovery.

While the Obama administration continued to stimulate the U.S. economy—through the Recovery and Reinvestment Act of 2009—George Osborne, the new British Conservative chancellor, pursued a modified Hayekian experiment. The government set out to slash public expenditure by £99 billion—or 7 per cent of GDP—per year by the 2015–2016 fiscal year and increase taxes by another £29 billion per year.

Two years later, the score card is in. Since May 2010, when U.S. and British fiscal policy diverged, the U.S. economy has grown—albeit slowly. The British economy is currently contracting. Unemployment in the United States has gone down by 1.4 percentage points; in Britain, it has gone up by 0.2 percentage points. And despite keeping up stimulus measures, the Obama administration has been more successful in reducing the government deficit—by 2.5 percentage points compared with Osborne's 1.9 percentage points.

Earlier this year, Paul Krugman wrote that "Britain . . . was supposed to be a showcase for 'expansionary austerity,' the notion that instead of increasing government spending to fight recessions, you should slash spending instead—and that this would lead to faster economic growth." But, as Krugman wrote, "it turns out that . . . Britain is doing worse this time than it did during the Great Depression."

For Keynesians, this is not surprising: By cutting its spending, the government is also cutting its income. Austerity policies have plunged most European economies (including Britain's) into double-dip recessions. At last, opinion is starting to shift—but too slowly and too late to save the world from years of stagnation.

32. The Olympics should have taught us the benefits of picking winners
Project Syndicate | June 22, 2012

As Olympic mania swept the world in recent weeks, it transported the host country, Great Britain, to a rare display of public exultation. Indeed, the successes of "Team GB" produced an upsurge of patriotic rejoicing akin to victory in war. Britain finished third in the gold medal count, behind the United States and China, much larger countries, but ahead of Russia, which traditionally competes with America for first place.

So, what is the secret of Olympic success? The acquisition of medals, precisely because it gives so much satisfaction, has become the object of scientific inquiry and national endeavor. Before the 2012 Games, the *Financial Times* combined four economic models to produce the following "consensus" prediction of gold medals (the actual results are in brackets): 1. United States, 39 (46); 2. China, 37 (38); 3. Great Britain, 24 (29); 4. Russia, 12 (24); 5. South Korea, 12 (13); and 6. Germany, 9 (11). The gold medal rankings and overall medal placement (gold, silver, and bronze) were correctly predicted in all cases.

The most striking finding is that the medal count can be predicted with great accuracy from four key variables: population, GDP per capita, past performance, and host status. Everything else – different training structures, better equipment, and so forth – is pretty much noise.

The impact of population and GDP is obvious: A large population increases the chance that a country will have athletes with the natural talent to win medals, and a high GDP means that it will have the money to invest in the infrastructure and training needed to develop medal-winning athletes.

Past performance is also important: the visibility and prestige of a sport increases after Olympic success, as does funding. Medals attract money; failure results in cuts.

Finally, the "home advantage" includes not just the benefit of morale and the opportunity to train in the actual Olympic venues, but also the funding boost that host status brings. In 2004, British athletes received £70 million ($110 million). By 2008, after London was awarded the 2012 Games, the total was £245 million, and stood at £264 million this year. Over the past ten Olympics, the host country has won 54 per cent more medals on average than when it was not the host. Hosting the Olympics boosts performance before the hosted Games, and has effects that outlast them.

Some sports are more sensitive to income and host-nation effects than others. Equestrianism, sailing, cycling, and swimming, for example, are far more expensive than running, and this reduces the participation of low-income countries. It is almost impossible for some countries to produce medal-winning athletes in some sports – Ethiopia has only one swimming pool per six million people.

Sometimes, poor countries are priced out of a sport. India was historically strong at field hockey, winning almost all of the gold medals between 1928 and 1968, but, since the Games switched from grass to expensive synthetic turf, the Indians have won just one field hockey medal. Some of the sports at which Britain has done particularly well, like cycling and rowing, are most highly influenced by income and host effects.

Brazil can therefore expect to improve considerably on its modest haul (15 medals) and 21st-place finish when it hosts the 2016 Games. As for the others, the formula for success is fairly simple: select your potentially winning sports, pick the potential medalists in those sports, pour money into them, and stick with both the sports and the players until the medals roll in. The funding can be corporate sponsorship (as in the United States), state money (as in China), or a mixture of National Lottery and state money (as in the United Kingdom).

Two questions arise. First, why should a country concentrate on accumulating trophies at the expense of other desirable goods? And, second, can the formula for "picking winners" in sports be replicated for competitive success in international trade?

The answer to the first is not obvious. An economist would probably argue that money spent on education, housing, and health care brings more "welfare" than money spent in the quest for medals. When all is said and done, sports are entertainment; the others are necessities.

But that argument ignores the effect of sporting success on national morale, an intangible factor in a country's success in other, more "serious," spheres of endeavor. A country that can succeed in one sphere of peaceful competition is encouraged to feel that it can do well in others.

One can treat this claim with a certain degree of skepticism – after all, the 2004 Athens Olympics failed to produce a Greek economic miracle. But it does lead to the second question: Can the methods that produce Olympic winners be applied elsewhere?

Nothing is more discredited in Anglo-American economics than the policy of "picking winners." The consensus has been that it inevitably leads to the state "backing losers." Economic success, on this view, is best left to the unfettered play of market forces.

This philosophy has been heavily jolted by two inconvenient facts: the financial collapse of 2007-2008 and the experience of countries like Japan, South Korea, Taiwan, Germany, and even the US, where economic success depended heavily on sustained government investment of the kind that has produced Olympic medals. As in sports, so in economic life: government commitment can start a virtuous circle of success, while government neglect can trigger a vicious circle of decline.

Nevertheless, the popular hunger for sporting success, and the celebratory outpouring that it evokes, is bound to provoke some disquiet. It seems to mark humanity's retreat into infantilism. But if the douceur of sports can channel aggressive passions into benign, if trivial pursuits, why should we deny our star performers their heroic stature?

33a. Go left... Go right... Go downhill.
New Statesman | September 23, 2012

Refreshed by his summer holiday, David Cameron vowed to "get Britain moving again". A slew of kick-starting initiatives has followed, most of them the brainchild of his government's one-man think tank, Vince Cable.

The figures are dire. After a tepid recovery from the collapse of 2008, the British economy has started shrinking again. Most forecasters expect a negative growth outcome for this year. The same is true of the eurozone.

What has gone wrong? In the spring of 2009 all the major economies, including Britain's, were given a large fiscal and monetary stimulus. Then in June 2010 George Osborne, the Chancellor, entered the Treasury with a large dose of austerity. It is true that a correlation isn't a cause, but could it be that the earlier recovery had something to do with the stimulus, and the subsequent decline with the austerity? At any rate these are striking coincidences. By contrast, the United States, which escaped Dr Osborne's cure, has continued to grow, albeit feebly.

It would be foolish to say that Osborne's budgets have caused the slump. The charge is that his budgets, far from offsetting, have aggravated the collapse of demand that followed the banking crash of 2008. Austerity has not caused the economy to shrink, but has kept it from recovering. Meanwhile, it is wonderful to see how we clutch at straws. For example, the fall in retail sales in July compared to July last year has been attributed to people preferring to watch the London Olympics rather than go shopping. Could it just be that they had less disposable income than last year? Then there was the Queen's Diamond Jubilee. This was blamed for the poor second-quarter showing. In a healthy economy, however, parties don't typically lead to such severe hangovers.

The government clutches at straws of its own. The Prime Minister and the Chancellor assert ad nauseam that Britain's recovery was derailed by the eurozone crisis. Unfortunately, the dates are wrong. The British recovery petered out before the eurozone crisis started. It actually petered out as soon as the coalition got started.

Yet surely it was only the government's austerity policy that prevented Britain from going the way of those big European spenders? Here is David Cameron in the *Mail on Sunday* (2 September): "When I became Prime Minister our market interest rates were the same as Spain's. Ours are now less than 2 per cent; theirs more than 6 per cent. Why? Because we threw a lifeline around the British economy and pulled it back from the cliff edge."

But wait a minute: Spain had a budget surplus and a low public debt in the run-up to the crisis. Since then Spain has followed much the same austerity policy as the UK. So how can the difference in the yields of the two governments' debt be due to the differences in their fiscal policies? There must be "other factors".

Now we come to some good news. "Yes, growth has been disappointing," Cameron admits, "but in the past two years we've also seen more than 900,000 jobs created in the private sector." This may be true, but the number we are most interested in is net, not gross, employment. In fact, unemployment has risen in the two years of coalition rule, from 2.48 million to 2.59 million. More importantly, almost half of the new jobs created under Cameron are part-time. Agreed, better some employment than no employment, but hardly the resounding success story it's made out to be.

There is still a puzzle. The government takes comfort from unemployment having fallen recently, even though the economy has continued to shrink. The headline figure of 2.59 million unemployed is actually slightly lower than it was six months ago. The reason for this is almost certainly that employers are hanging on to skilled labour for fear of losing it altogether, with the consequence that there has been a fall in recorded productivity. As the *Guardian* put it, ". . . it now requires many more of us to labour away to churn out the reduced volume of stuff" (15 August).

The figures have to be spun to disguise Osborne's failure. The present situation is the predictable and, by some of us, predicted outcome of policies of fiscal austerity pursued in the face of the worst economic crisis since the Second World War. That prediction rests on a straightforward Keynesian analysis.

Keynes explained how conditions of semi-slump can get established. Let's start from a situation of full employment and high private indebtedness. This latter does not matter so long as the economy is growing. But suddenly the next step up the ladder is no longer there and a lot of people find themselves "living beyond their means".

The only thing they can do is to reduce their spending: that is, save more. But what happens if all households and firms try to increase their saving at the same time? Well, then the total spending in the economy will fall because everyone's spending is someone else's income. There will be less demand for goods and services and therefore for labour. Our collective attempts to get back into balance – get rid of our credit-card debt, as the Prime Minister likes to put it – will have made us all poorer, and, indeed, reduced the amount of saving as well, given that we will have smaller incomes out of which to save. So the economy will go on shrinking until the excess saving is eliminated by the growing poverty of the community.

The essence of this insight is captured in the phrase the "fallacy of composition". The fallacy consists in the claim that what is true of the parts must also be true for the whole. The best-known application of this fallacy is the "paradox of thrift". New acts of saving, though virtuous for the individual, make us all poorer when the demand for new capital has declined.

That is why Keynes rejected more saving as the remedy for a slump. The correct response was more spending. And if private agents lack the resources or incentive to increase their spending then the government needs to increase its own spending. This, in a nutshell, is the theory of the stimulus.

We all worry about debt, yet the important figure is not what I owe but the ratio of what I owe to my income. I can try to reduce this ratio either by saving my income to pay off the debt or trying to make my income larger. Reducing the national debt is more complicated. It can only be done by taxing more or spending less, and this drives down people's incomes and creates unemployment. Furthermore, by reducing incomes, it also reduces people's ability to pay taxes, and this can be self-defeating. Something like this has happened in Europe, where falling incomes due to austerity have driven debt ratios up, not down.

Offloading private debt on to the public sector may help stabilise the economy, but does not, of itself, produce recovery; and may, in addition, frighten the bond markets into raising their default premium on government paper.

So we seem to be between a rock and a hard place. International organisations such as the OECD and the IMF are more or less agreed that the present austerity policies are preventing growth; but they offer no alternatives. Here is Ángel Gurría of the OECD: "Deleveraging necessarily means higher savings, and that means lower consumption and therefore lower demand. And the lower demand means even lower employment and even lower incomes for households and lower revenues from governments. And both of these mean slower deleveraging. It is a vicious circle."

And here is the latest IMF study: "The recovery has stalled and unemployment is still too high . . . Additional macroeconomic easing is needed to close the output gap faster. Scaling back fiscal tightening plans should be the main policy lever if growth does not build momentum by early 2013 even after further monetary stimulus and strong credit easing measures."

To a Keynesian, these belated insights are hardly news. Gurría, for instance, is merely repeating Keynes's argument that to withdraw demand from an already demand-deficient economy will lead not to recovery, but to a shrinking economy, a growing debt (private and public) and the need for more austerity.

Today there is a silent U-turn going on in the UK as well as in eurozone countries, hence Cameron's call to "cut through the dither". But there is still great disagreement about what the recovery policy should be.

The debate is broadly between the supply-siders and the demand-siders. The supply-siders argue that there is too little money in the economy, the demand-siders that there is too little spending power. It might seem that the two come to the same thing, but as Keynes pointed out, the holder of money has a choice: whether to "hoard" it or spend it. Those who argue that any increase in the money supply is bound to be spent on buying goods and services ignore the existence of "liquidity preference" – the desire to hold on to cash because of uncertainty about the future.

The favourite tool of supply-side expansionism is quantitative easing (QE), or "printing money". Ben Bernanke of the Federal Reserve and Mervyn King of the Bank of England, together the most powerful central bank governors today, believe that the reason the Great Depression of the 1930s was so deep and lasted so long was that the monetary authorities allowed the money supply to collapse. They are determined not to make the same mistake this time. The technique of printing money is for the central bank to buy government (and possibly corporate) securities from non-financial companies and give them cash in return. The recipients deposit this additional cash in their bank accounts. They then spend it buying assets. Alternatively, the banks' increased cash reserves enable them to reduce the rates they charge for loans. Either way, there is a stimulus to spending.

Despite attempts by the Bank of England to devise "more economically relevant" measures of money, the evidence is that only a small fraction of the "new money" has got out into the economy, enough to stop a slide all the way down into another Great Depression, but not enough to produce a recovery. The main benefit of QE has been to keep down the cost of government borrowing: one of the inestimable advantages of having your own central bank able to print money. This gives the government more room for fiscal manoeuvre.

So, contrary to Cameron's claim, it is not fiscal austerity that has kept the cost of government borrowing low, but QE – plus the lack of business confidence in alternative investment prospects.

The government has dangled a succession of carrots before the banks to induce them to "lend more" of the extra money they are getting. In March, there was a National Loan Guarantee Scheme. This was replaced less than six months later by the Funding for Lending Scheme. However, attempts to increase the volume of lending by lowering banks' funding costs have largely failed. Since July, when the new scheme was launched, bank funding costs have fallen by 0.5 per cent, but the rate for new mortgages has fallen by only 0.1 per cent; that is to say, the spread between the two has in fact widened, to the great advantage of banks' balance sheets, but not borrowers. Now the government has promised a £40bn guarantee for private infrastructure investment. These schemes all help, yet the basic problem is not too little credit, but too little demand for credit. Would people borrow more, even at lower interest rates, when the economy is shrinking? As economists used to say, "You can't push on a string."

The alternative expansionary tool is an increase in the government deficit. Instead of the Bank of England buying bonds, the government sells bonds – that is, incurs debt – to finance its spending. There would be no point in doing this if the private sector was already investing its money productively. If, in this situation, the government started selling more of its debt, it would merely "crowd out" existing private investment. Yet this is not the case when there is a deficiency of aggregate spending. Government borrowing then absorbs "idle" savings and puts them to use.

There are many ways it can do this. The least promising is the policy of tax cuts for the rich advocated by the political right. The reason is that the rich save more of their money than the poor, so the stimulating effect may be quite small; and the non-saved part of the tax windfall is quite likely to go into the kind of financial and real-estate speculation that precipitated the last crash. Tax reductions for the poor, though, in the form of temporary relief from National Insurance contributions, would be helpful.

In the present situation there are two quick ways for the government to boost total spending. It could supply all households with time-limited spending vouchers – a Christmas present of, say, £100 for each family in the land. Some of the extra spending power would be used to buy imported goods or repay debt, but there would still be some net increase in domestic spending.

On the investment side, the easiest thing that the government could do would be to reinstate capital spending programmes cancelled in the drive for deficit reduction, with social housing and school-building given priority. Easing planning regulations (a favourite supply-side measure) to stimulate construction will help, but the private sector will not construct buildings if there is no effective demand for them.

The government should also set up a national investment bank with its own portfolio of investment projects focused on infrastructure and cutting-edge technology. A firm, long-term commitment by the investment bank would not only give the country new roads and energy sources but spread jobs to small and medium-sized suppliers.

The crucial difference between the National Investment Bank and the government's plan to guarantee £40bn of private infrastructure projects is that the investment bank would be an active investor with its own funds, whereas the government's plan leaves the initiative to the private sector. Even Vince Cable's so-called small business bank is not expected to do more than "shake up the market in business finance". This is based on the fallacious doctrine that the private sector will always be better at "picking winners" than any public authority, however shielded an authority may be from political interference. This largely reflects the failed experiments of the 1960s, such as British Leyland. The experience of many European and Asian countries gives the lie to the notion that state-led investment is bound to fail. And the recent catastrophic performance of the financial services industry should guard us from the belief that the private sector always knows best.

The important requirement, as our success in the Olympics showed, is the identification of potential winners and sticking with them long enough to show results. The bane of British "industrial policy" has been not the inability of public authorities to pick winners, but the chopping and changing of policy in response to temporary financial exigencies. The cancellation of public capital projects after 2008 is a good example of this unsteadiness of aim.

This is where the economic debate rests. It is high time to move it from academic discussion to the political arena. This will be necessary in any case if, as I believe, the prospect under present policy is for semi-permanent continuation of conditions of semi-slump.

33b. When the facts change, should I change my mind?
Vince Cable
New Statesman | March 6, 2013

The British economy is still operating at levels around or below those before the 2008 financial crisis and roughly 15 per cent below an albeit unsustainable pre-crisis trend. There was next to no growth during 2012 and the prospect for 2013 is of very modest recovery.

Unsurprisingly there is vigorous debate as to what has gone wrong. And also what has gone right; unemployment has fallen as a result of a million (net) new jobs in the private sector and there is vigorous growth of new enterprises. Optimistic official growth forecasts and prophets of mass unemployment have both been confounded.

Arguments about growth and recovery involve different timescales. I share the view, set out well by the LSE Growth Commission, that long-term growth involves a major and sustained commitment to skills, innovation and infrastructure investment. However, we are also currently below trend growth and below capacity.

Two years ago, I responded in the *New Statesman* to Robert Skidelsky's Keynesian critique of government economic policies. He returned to the charge in the *NS* in September 2012. His contribution has been to lift the dispiritingly low level of public debate about UK economic policy by drawing on the great work of Keynes, of whom he is the definitive biographer and whose disciples taught me economics.

Skidelsky's central observation is the "striking coincidence" between what he describes as the coalition's "large dose of austerity" and a period of what he calls "semi-slump". He is sufficiently gracious and well informed to state that it is "foolish to say that [George] Osborne's budgets have caused the slump" – unlike the Labour front bench, which has had no such inhibitions. His complaint is a more subtle one: that "austerity . . . has kept [the economy] from recovering".

Economic populism

In the political bearpit the arguments are less sophisticated. Keynes's name is often used to dignify any proposal that involves the government spending more money and any opposition to cuts.

This crude Keynesianism sidesteps the causes and effects of the financial crisis, including the drag on growth from damaged banks; as well as other structural problems, such as skills shortages and a long-standing neglect of vital exporting industries, which our national industrial strategy is now trying to address.

In opposition to the cruder "demand-side" arguments are some equally crude "supplyside" arguments, which trace an ancestral link to another of the 20th-century greats, Friedrich Hayek (or the Austrian school more generally). This bastardised supply-side economics often degenerates into a saloonbar whine about HSE inspectors, newts and birds that block new development, bloodyminded workers, equalities legislation and Eurocrats who dream up regulations for square tomatoes and straight bananas. Philosophical cover is provided by the belief that the private sector can always fill the space left by a retreating state.

An eclectic approach

Neither set of prejudices does justice to the complexities of the crisis that has submerged the UK (and other western countries) in deep economic water. A variety of approaches is relevant. Worryingly, few economists beyond Hyman Minsky and Charles Kindleberger have really addressed the phenomenon of financial mania and banking collapses (although Ben Bernanke, the chairman of the Federal Reserve, produced important work on how the banking crisis worsened the Great Depression in the US). Another defining feature of the present crisis has been the accumulation of a large volume of household debt, mostly linked to mortgages, which, as Irving Fisher argued a century ago, leads to "debt deflation", with a downward spiral of depressed demand, unserviceable debt and weak confidence. Then Milton Friedman understood the importance of money supply in the interwar slump, which has played out in the current crisis in activist, unorthodox monetary policy. And largely ignored in our parochial policy squabbles has been the impact of the rapidly shifting centre of gravity of the world economy towards emerging markets and the impact of this change on capital flows and demand, shifting the terms of trade – mainly through oil – against commodity importers. None of these issues makes Keynes irrelevant, but they suggest the need for a more complex and eclectic framework for analysis.

Skidelsky reminds us of the principal elements of Keynes's ideas which are relevant. Economic slump is not self-correcting: there may be a deficiency in aggregate demand resulting in spare capacity – the so-called output gap; there can be limits to the effectiveness of monetary policy in dealing with such a deficiency; and there is an important role to be played by active fiscal policy in stimulating demand.

The Keynesian framework was, however, developed in a different context from the present. It is essentially relevant to one country in slump acting in isolation (the assumption in the General Theory, 1936) or to a world that is collectively in slump. The world faced collective slump in the post-1929 crash and it did so again in 2009 when a Keynesian response was required (and was forthcoming) during a brief global recession. The eurozone may now approximate to these conditions and requires collective (German-led) reflation. But Britain is not part of that problem, though affected by it. In the UK, too, certain sectors are being severely affected by lack of demand, notably construction. All in all, the present evidence does indeed – with qualifications – point to some weakness of domestic demand and a low risk of expansionary policies spilling over into significant domestically generated inflation.

There is, however, no global problem of aggregate demand. World trade grew by almost 14 per cent in 2010, 5 per cent in 2011 and perhaps 3 per cent in 2012. The gross domestic product of emerging markets has on the whole grown fast. To be sure, it is not a simple matter to convert Blockbuster checkout staff into workers exporting Jaguars or their parts to China. But whatever the problem is, it is not a deficiency of global aggregate demand – we need only look at the behaviour of commodity markets since mid- 2010 to realise that.

Keynes, of course, fully understood the importance of international trade and in the 1929-31 period fought a bitter battle over the Gold Standard, which had led to British exports being overpriced and unable to grow on the international markets. That pattern does not exist today. The pound devalued by over 20 per cent in real, trade-weighted terms in 2008/2009 and has remained roughly in that position. As a small country (with 3 per cent of global GDP) with more price-competitive tradable products, the UK should benefit from rapidly growing exports, and that is beginning to happen in the big emerging markets.

Banks and the crisis

There is another respect in which the Keynesian model does not deal with the central event in the current crisis – the banking collapse. Skidelsky does not mention it, even in passing. This is a little like trying to explain the disappearance of the dinosaurs while assuming away the asteroid.

The banking system hardly rates a mention in the General Theory: not surprising, as the British banking system, unlike America's, was stable in the 1930s. To seek precedents for the present position, we need to look at early-19th-century Britain or the recent experience in Japan. A seminal paper by Carmen Reinhart and Kenneth Rogoff suggests that financial crises are typically followed by slow and difficult recovery.

There are several specific factors which reinforce that conclusion for the UK. The UK had the biggest banking sector (assets relative to GDP) of any major country. The financial sector, and the associated bubble in property prices, was relied on to provide a substantial contribution to government revenue. Its demise led to a "structural" deficit, estimated (in 2010) at roughly 6 per cent of GDP. Unlike the Treasury in the interwar period, which insisted on balanced budgets, the coalition government has been Keynesian in approaching fiscal policy in a broadly counter-cyclical manner by letting stabilisers operate. The policy issue is how to address the structural deficit: a problem closer to that of a developing country whose leading commodity export has collapsed and which has to persuade creditors to finance growing sovereign debt until structural budget and wider economic reform has been completed in a credible time frame. Keynesian economics does not provide much insight into such problems.

Furthermore, the damage inflicted on the banking system has severely impaired credit flows, especially to small and medium-sized companies and to infrastructure project fin - ancing. The money transmission mechanism has been badly disrupted, which blunts not only monetary policy but also fiscal policy, by reducing the income multiplier and accelerator by which demand is translated into increased production and investment. Any reliable escape route from the crisis has to have a plausible mechanism for boosting credit to business, especially SMEs. That is why I am working in the government to launch a state-backed business bank and promote non-bank finance.

The supply side

This credit supply problem is sometimes seen as part of a wider "supply-side" criticism that pumping demand into a supply-constrained economy is – in an extreme case – pointless because it will spill over into inflation or imports. The caricature may be wrong but there is some reason for these concerns. Again, analogies with developing countries are relevant. Past attempts to use crude deficit financing to deal with chronic underemployment have been unsuccessful because of such structural problems.

Nonetheless I have no doubt that there is some scope for more demand to boost output, particularly if the stimulus is targeted on supply bottlenecks such as infrastructure and skills. And, like me, Skidelsky believes that state-led banking could simultaneously ease credit and other supply constraints while stimulating demand. He is right that these factors can interact. But, as the ministerial promoter of two such banks (the Green Investment Bank and the Business Bank),

I am painfully conscious that progressing quickly from millions to billions is not straightforward. There are EU state aid clearance rules. Projects require careful planning and due diligence.

Numbers are relevant here. Michael Stewart's 1968 book *Keynes and After* argues that Keynes was assuming income multipliers of two to three in the General Theory – which is why he saw fiscal policy as so powerful. The Office for Budget Responsibility estimates multipliers in the present context to be much lower: 0.4 for tax cuts and government current spending and 1.0 for capital projects. The International Monetary Fund uses figures of 0.9 to 1.7 (but these include international linkages). This suggests that if fiscal policy is to work in a Keynesian manner, it needs to be targeted carefully, concentrating on capital projects.

Active monetary policy

Skidelsky uses a Keynesian framework to criticise the coalition's economic policies in two main respects: he argues that cuts in government spending (with increased VAT) since May 2010 – "austerity" – undermined growth and economic recovery; and that attempts to sustain demand through monetary rather than fiscal policy have been ineffectual, as Keynes would have predicted.

To deal with monetary policy first: it has indeed been the first line of defence in the crisis, not only in the UK but in the US (and the eurozone) and under the last government as well as this. So, naturally, monetary policy has been a necessary complement to deficit reduction. Interest rates were cut aggressively; short-term policy rates have been near zero for four years now: negative in real terms. In addition, QE or quantitative easing – gilt purchases by the central bank –has been used extensively and although the mechanism is a source of debate it is widely believed to have stimulated demand and activity through low long-term interest rates, higher asset prices and exchange-rate depreciation.

Keynes fully recognised the importance of utilising monetary policy to counter deflation. In particular, he emphasised low long-term interest rates to encourage investment. He would have understood the monetary policy adopted now. And interwar experience – as documented by Professor Nick Crafts in particular – was far more positive than recognised at the time. In a speech to the Guildhall last year, I drew on this parallel to support expansionary monetary policy. Keynes's concern was that there were limits to monetary policy. In particular, interest rates could not go below zero. Today's problem is more complex. Negative official real rates coexist with high lending rates charged by the banks, especially to SMEs. Indeed, the low level of risk-free rates, including our very low gilt yields, actually indicate how monetary conditions have been tight for the greater part of the economy.

Money growth has been low and nominal spending growth in the economy weaker in the past five years than in any other years of our history. Low gilt yields indicate how risk-free government paper becomes an attractive investment in these circumstances, as an alternative rather than a boost to private sector investment.

The role of QE

There has been growing criticism of QE in western countries, partly on the grounds that it may have diminishing returns but mainly because of undesirable side effects: the impact on pension funds and the distributional consequences of boosting asset prices (benefiting the asset-wealthy). The argument is building that QE may have been useful in the accident and emergency ward but is less useful for long-term rehab. Long-term savers are right to be concerned – yet this merely reinforces how important it is to return the UK to growth and the higher long-term rates that usually follow growth. A premature rate rise would achieve the opposite.

There is currently a pause in QE in the UK and two related ideas are being developed to sustain loose monetary policy. The first is for the central bank to acquire a wider range of assets, from corporate loans to infrastructure project bonds. By taking risk off the private-sector balance sheet, we encourage it to find new investments. This is surely sensible. However, Mervyn King, the present governor of the Bank of England, regards such interventions as being akin to fiscal policy, in effect replacing government borrowing. To that extent, the debate about fiscal v monetary policy ceases to be one of theory or principle but a more mundane question of statistical classification.

The second idea gaining currency worldwide is to recognise the legitimacy of aggressive monetary policy by changing the mandate of the central bank to incorporate growth in some form as well as inflation. This idea has gained more prominence as people have begun to realise how, before the crisis, Consumer Prices Index inflation hid serious asset (namely, housing) inflation and how, after the banking crisis and with conditions generally depressed, it was not always a useful or accurate regulator of the macroeconomy on its own. In 2011 in particular, the UK economy suffered several negative shocks, notably from fluctuations in oil prices and the European sovereign debt crises. Growth of the UK economy required aggressively easier policy, but because of the mandated focus on CPI, several members of the Bank of England's Monetary Policy Committee were calling for rates to rise.

So, there are voices asking whether there is scope to be more flexible. On the other hand, inflation targeting helped produce a decade of relative stability for the UK economy and is well understood by the public, so the bar for any change must be high.

Whoever is in government, the UK is probably facing years of fiscal consolidation – so it is essential for the monetary levers to be working well. Keynes may have been right about how difficult monetary policy is at the zero bound, but the first priority must be for it to do no harm, and crucially for it not to snuff out any incipient recovery by tightening inappropriately.

Did austerity kill growth?

The other criticism is that fiscal tightening has more than offset loose monetary policy, killing recovery. This is an empirical question. The evidence is not straightforward. Some of the crucial concepts, such as the "output gap" or the "structural deficit", are difficult to quantify with any precision.

Nonetheless, the data does not support the conclusion that deficit reduction has had dramatic effects on the economy. There has been only modest reduction in the budget deficit, partly because the government has been allowing counter-cyclical stabilisers to operate, and partly because we have taken the conscious decision not to introduce further cuts at a time when the weaker economy has damaged tax revenues.

The OBR has looked at the contributory factors explaining poor growth performance in the past two years. It suggests that the main factor weakening the economy has been low private consumption, caused by a squeeze in real wages, caused in turn by inflation in global commodity prices as well as higher import prices following devaluation (in 2011 sterling commodity prices rose 6 per cent for food and 15 per cent for oil). The slowdown in the eurozone has played a role latterly, hitting confidence.

Public investment

What is also clear, however, is that the part of the fiscal consolidation achieved through reduced capital spending has had economic consequences. The OBR itself saw capital investment as having the highest multiplier of all government spending, even before the IMF sharply upgraded its own estimates. The present government has partially reversed the Labour cuts – the autumn statement of 2011 produced £5bn more investment in transport – but without doubt this is the least efficient form of fiscal tightening. It can inflict more damage on output than cuts in current spending or tax increases because the multipliers are much higher. We inherited from Labour a severe cyclical downturn in construction, caused by the collapse of private housebuilding and commercial property development. It has had the effect of reducing supply capability as well as demand (because infrastructure is neglected and the skills of workers in the construction industry have been allowed to degrade).

The coalition government acknowledged these problems in the 2012 Autumn Statement by boosting government investment (and simultaneously top-slicing current spending), yet the increase was modest (£5bn) and in the short run it has little effect on demand because it takes time to organise capital projects. With this increase, public sector net investment is now higher as a proportion of GDP, under the coalition, than it was between 1997 and 2010. Nevertheless, one obvious question is why capital investment cannot now be greatly expanded. Pessimists say that the central government is incapable of mobilising capital investment quickly. But that is absurd: only five years ago the government was managing to build infrastructure, schools and hospitals at a level £20bn higher than last year. Businesses are forward-thinking and react to a future pipe - line of activity, regardless of how "shovelready" it may be: we have seen that in energy investment, where the major firms need certainty over decades.

The more controversial question is whether the government should not switch but should borrow more, at current very low interest rates, in order to finance more capital spending: building of schools and colleges; small road and rail projects; more prudential borrowing by councils for housebuilding. This last is crucial to reviving an area which led economic recovery in the 1930s but is now severely depressed. Such a programme would inject demand into the weakest sector of our economy – construction – and, at one remove, the manufacturing supply chain (cement, steel). It would target two significant bottlenecks to growth: infrastructure and housing.

Yet nobody knows how the markets might respond. While low interest rates are often an encouragement to invest more, they are also an indication of great uncertainty. But more investment is what the more traditional Keynesians are now arguing for (and essentially what Skidelsky is saying, stripped of the invective).

Such a strategy does not undermine the central objective of reducing the structural deficit, and may assist it by reviving growth. It may complicate the secondary objective of reducing government debt relative to GDP because it entails more state borrowing; but in a weak economy, more public investment increases the numerator and the denominator.

Because the government has wisely issued debt with a long maturity, we suffer less from the risks of a debt spiral, where refinancing maturing debt rapidly becomes impossible. Consequently, the effect on our fiscal situation of higher interest rates is in fact nowhere near as bad as having weak growth.

Why not? The orthodox view has been that higher borrowing (and therefore debt) in the short term will excite the markets, with unpredictable consequences for borrowing costs. Higher borrowing rates are a deadweight that the Treasury would quite sensibly want to avoid, particularly if they knock on to higher rates for heavily indebted private-sector borrowers. At a time when mortgage borrowers are enjoying record low rates, this would be quite a blow.

Balance of risks

Contrary to the rhetoric around economic policy, the real disagreements have had little to do with ideology or economic theory. The government has happily deployed Keynesian techniques where feasible – as in its counter-cyclical fiscal policy. It has been sufficiently pragmatic to allow the fiscal consolidation to drift from four years to seven. The question throughout has been how to maintain the confidence of creditors when the government is having to borrow at historically exceptional levels, without killing confidence in the economy in so doing through too harsh an approach.

When the government was formed it was in the context of febrile markets and worries about sovereign risk, at that stage in Greece, but with the potential for contagion. There was good reason to worry that the UK, as the country arguably most damaged by the banking crisis and with the largest fiscal deficit in the G20, could lose the confidence of creditors without a credible plan for deficit reduction including an early demonstration of commitment.

Almost three years later, the question is whether the balance of risks has changed. The IMF argued last May that the risk of losing market confidence as a result of a more relaxed approach to fiscal policy – particularly the financing of more capital investment by borrowing – may have diminished relative to the risk of public finances deteriorating as a consequence of continued lack of growth.

On the balance of risks, there is no "right" or "wrong" answer. There is no theoretically correct solution: rather, a matter of judgement – which incorporates a political assessment of which risk is the least palatable. There is a body of opinion arguing that the risks to the economy of sticking to existing plans are greater than the risks stemming from significantly increased and sustained public investment targeted at those areas of the economy where there are severe impediments to growth (housing; skills; infrastructure; innovation). But this is also too crude and binary a characterisation of the position; the government has carried out considerable policy reform in these areas, not least in my own department, the fruits of which take a while to mature. The balance of risks remains a matter of judgement.

34. Infrastructure Bill Speech
House of Lords | October 25, 2012

My Lords, as someone who has never been averse to having a go at the Chancellor of the Exchequer, I start by saying how idiotic and puerile it is for newspapers to make a lead story of which ticket he used for his journey from Chester to London. It is George Osborne's stewardship of the economy, not his travel arrangements, which deserves censure. However, we have an infantile press.

Three big mistakes stick out over the past two and a half years. The first was the belief that cutting down government spending would automatically produce recovery. I know the Government now claim that they never believed anything so simple or idiotic, but they did, and there is plenty of evidence to prove it. Austerity is not a recovery policy.

The second has been the Chancellor's failure to distinguish between current and capital spending. This has made the deficit seem more dangerous than it was. The prime example of this blind spot was the £50 billion cut in capital spending. The consequences of this for the construction industry and for house, transport, education and hospital building have been devastating.

The third was the Chancellor's belief that without a severe fiscal contraction Britain would go the way of Greece: that is, interest rates would go through the roof. This was doubly wrong. First, with an independent central bank able to buy government debt in whatever quantities were needed there was never any chance of gilt yields rising to the levels experienced by Greece, Portugal, Ireland and Spain. Secondly, and perhaps even more importantly, a reduction in the cost of government borrowing is no guarantee of a reduction in the cost of commercial loans sufficient to offset the collapse of the private demand for loans.

All three mistakes were interrelated parts of the wrong theory of the economy. Anyone who is interested in economics must start the analysis there. I am not going to go into it, but it is well known to those who are economically literate. The results have been zero growth since George Osborne took office. That was entirely predictable and was predicted by some of us. I have been saying for two and a half years-and I am not alone-that austerity would not produce growth and it has not produced growth. Now the international agencies are saying the same thing. Slowly but surely, the Government are being driven to plan B, though the Prime Minister prefers to call it plan A-plus.

It is against that background that I give a cautious welcome to the proposals in this Bill. Better late than never, better too little than nothing at all. As I understand it, the Bill aims to do three things. First, it provides for the Government to guarantee up to £40 billion of "nationally significant" private infrastructure investments which have to be ready to start within 12 months of the guarantee. As the Treasury explains it, the aim is, "to kick start critical infrastructure projects that may have stalled because of adverse credit conditions".

That is Treasury language. The guarantees might cover key project risks such as construction, performance or revenue.

Secondly, the Government will lend money directly to private investors to enable 30 public/private partnership projects worth £6 billion to go ahead in the next 12 months; I do not think that has been mentioned yet in the debate. Finally, a £5 billion export financing facility will be available later this year to overseas buyers of British capital goods; in other words, an export credit guarantee scheme of the type we are all familiar with. Having cancelled about £50 billion of certain public capital spending, the Government are hoping to replace it with an equivalent amount of private capital spending, much of which will never happen. That is completely illogical.

The main difference between this Bill and the British investment bank, which I have been urging, is that my bank - I call it "my bank" because I feel a certain sense of paternity in the idea, having been floating it for the last three years - would actively raise money in the private markets for its own investment projects whereas UK Guarantees, the government scheme, merely provides some finance for projects initiated by the private sector. In other words, the government scheme is still governed by the ideology that the private sector is more likely to pick winners than a state investment bank and that that is sufficient justification for waiting for the private sector to produce its projects.

There is no empirical evidence for it being true, as a general proposition, that the state is more likely to pick losers than the private sector. We have had many examples of that not being true. The economic collapse of 2008 is a very good one.

A mere guarantee for privately initiated schemes is bound to be less successful, apart from in the efficiency of the schemes, at securing the required volume of investment than a commitment by the Government to a definite infrastructure programme. So while I wish UK Guarantees well, a certain amount of scepticism is in order.

In the final part of my speech, I want to consider what is happening to the economy. When an economy is crawling along the bottom, any small wave is likely to lift our spirits. Over the past three quarters - that is, the past nine months - the economy has shrunk by 1 per cent. Even if, as now expected, it achieves a positive growth of about 0.8 per cent this quarter, that still leaves it in roughly the same place as it was a year ago. Moreover if, as commentators suggest, this boost is due to the Olympics, it will be in the nature of a windfall. However much we may rejoice in the achievements of our athletes, 28 gold medals is not enough to turn the British economy around.

However, there is still a puzzle, which is that unemployment has been static in the past few months, and even falling slightly, despite the fact that output is flat and the economically active population has increased by 550,000 over the past two years. You would therefore expect unemployment to have increased. Why has it not done so? That is the puzzle. There are several possible explanations, none of them conclusive, because the facts necessary for a convincing answer are buried in a labyrinth of tricky statistics and slippery definitions. It may be that employers have been hoarding labour, but that becomes less plausible the longer the recession goes on. Part of the answer at least must be that productivity - that is, output per hour worked - has been falling. As the *Guardian* put it, "it now requires many more of us to labour away to churn out the reduced volume of stuff". Falling productivity is just as serious a problem for the economy as rising unemployment, and a greater problem in the longer term.

The Prime Minister claims that 900,000 extra jobs have been created in the private sector over the past two years. I never know how many it is - sometimes it is 900,000 and sometimes it is 1 million; it goes up every day, but I am sticking to the 900,000 figure for the time being. That is not of course the net increase in jobs, given that 400,000 jobs have been lost in the public sector. The net increase in jobs has been 500,000.

Can the Minister tell us how many of the net gains in employment are full-time? Labour market statistics suggest that more than half of them are part-time or self-employed. Can the Minister also say whether those registered on government work programmes count in the Prime Minister's extra 900,000 private sector jobs?

The point is this: if a lot of the private sector job creation consists of part-time low-skilled jobs at the bottom end of the service sector, it would explain the decline in productivity that limits the rise in unemployment, but it is a poor omen for that vibrant, high-value economy that is supposed to secure our future prosperity.

I wish the Government well in these plans because I wish the country well, but we will need much more solid evidence than we have seen so far to believe that we have turned the corner and started to repair the damage of the past two and a half years.

35. One more chance for Osborne to change course
Financial Times | December 3, 2012

On Wednesday in his Autumn Statement George Osborne, the chancellor, is expected to admit that it will take three more years of austerity than originally planned to bring borrowing under control. Extravagant hopes are being placed on Mark Carney, the newly appointed Bank of England governor. There will be talk of an incipient recovery meeting "headwinds from the eurozone" and comfort will be taken from the thought that things could be a lot worse.

Of course, the crises in Europe and elsewhere have not helped. But the reasons for the failure of austerity and of quantitative easing to revive the economy lie deeper than headwinds. The chancellor's policy is based on the wrong theory of the economy; the BoE's on the wrong theory of money. Failure was predictable. This is not retrospective. A few of us who are proud to be Keynesians have been predicting failure for two years and more, before these headwinds appeared.

The Osborne recipe for recovery was based on the Treasury View, which Keynes confronted when arguing for public works during the Great Depression. The Treasury then argued that extra government spending would take away resources from the private sector; and even if there were spare resources, the loss of confidence and associated rise in long-term interest rates would far outweigh any stimulative effect of the extra spending.

Continuing the same line of thought, Mr Osborne's Treasury has argued that reduction in the deficit would "crowd in" the private sector by freeing up the capital and labour appropriated by the public sector and by "restoring confidence", so reducing long-term interest rates.

Keynes would have claimed otherwise: that cuts would reduce the level of total spending in the economy and thus perpetuate the slump. This has happened: the economy has been flat for two years and large parts of it outside London and the southeast are sinking.

The BoE's mistake has been to believe it is the supply of money that is critical for economic recovery; Keynes said it was the demand for money. In 1936 he wrote: "If, however, we are tempted to assert that money is the drink which stimulates the system to activity, we must remind ourselves that there may be several slips between the cup and the lip." These slips have been much in evidence. By printing money, the BoE aimed to increase spending through various channels: portfolio rebalancing, increased bank lending and, more vaguely, "confidence" that the BoE would not let the money supply collapse. But the money supply did collapse; some of the money has been invested in speculative assets; most of it remains stuck in banks and companies.

This does not come as a surprise to Keynesians. We have argued that banks create deposits in response to the demand for loans. The demand for loans depends on market expectations. If businesses see no market for their products, they will not borrow whatever the interest rate and the BoE cannot force them.

Unfortunately, both the Treasury and BoE are running out of ammunition. Mr Osborne has staked his credibility on the success of his deficit reduction programme. He has to go on pretending that foul is fair.

The BoE is fettered by its inflation target. The appointment of Mr Carney may be a masterstroke, however what the BoE needs is not a magician but a new mandate.

So where does that leave the economy? Without a change of policy it will not grow. And this is not just a temporary interruption of progress. The longer the economy remains stuck in semi-recession the weaker it becomes. Labour skills rust; the capital stock is not renewed. Each extra month the economy remains flat, its output potential is weakened.

What is to be done? If I were chancellor of the exchequer, I would immediately restore the programmes of capital investment cancelled by Mr Osborne and his predecessor Alistair Darling, accelerate infrastructure projects now in the pipeline and expand the programme of the Green Investment Bank. This would add about £100bn to aggregate demand, galvanising industrial supply chains.

The programme could be financed in various ways. I would borrow directly from the BoE for the government's own capital programmes. To allow for their monetary financing I would give the bank a new nominal income target of (say) 5 per cent to replace the existing target of 2 per cent inflation.

I would also set up a National Investment Bank, whose mandate would be to borrow from the pension and insurance funds for revenue-generating infrastructure projects, and which could offer a higher rate of return than obtainable from gilts.

Of course there are risks. These would be mitigated if the expansionary impulse could be co-ordinated with other countries. I would go to Brussels and seek agreement to a Europe-wide reversal of the austerity policy. But I would judge the risks of reversing austerity less than the risk of continuing policies that are slowly strangling our economic life.

36. Models Behaving Badly
Project Syndicate | December 18, 2012

"Why did no one see the crisis coming?" Queen Elizabeth II asked economists during a visit to the London School of Economics at the end of 2008. Four years later, the repeated failure of economic forecasters to predict the depth and duration of the slump would have elicited a similar question from the queen: Why the overestimate of recovery?

Consider the facts. In its 2011 forecast, the International Monetary Fund predicted that the European economy would grow by 2.1 per cent in 2012. In fact, it looks certain to shrink this year by 0.2 per cent. In the United Kingdom, the 2010 forecast of the Office for Budget Responsibility (OBR) projected 2.6 per cent growth in 2011 and 2.8 per cent growth in 2012; in fact, the UK economy grew by 0.9 per cent in 2011 and will flat-line in 2012. The OECD's latest forecast for eurozone GDP in 2012 is 2.3 per cent lower than its projection in 2010.

Likewise, the IMF now predicts that the European economy will be 7.8 per cent smaller in 2015 than it thought just two years ago. Some forecasters are more pessimistic than others (the OBR has a particularly sunny disposition), but no one, it seems, has been pessimistic enough.

Economic forecasting is necessarily imprecise: too many things happen for forecasters to be able to foresee all of them. So judgment calls and best guesses are an inevitable part of "scientific" economic forecasts.

But imprecision is one thing; the systematic overestimate of the economic recovery in Europe is quite another. Indeed, the figures have been repeatedly revised, even over quite short periods of time, casting strong doubt on the validity of the economic models being used. These models, and the institutions using them, rely on a built-in theory of the economy, which enables them to "assume" certain relationships. It is among these assumptions that the source of the errors must lie.

Two key mistakes stand out. The models used by all of the forecasting organizations dramatically underestimated the fiscal multiplier: the impact of changes in government spending on output. Second, they overestimated the extent to which quantitative easing (QE) by the monetary authorities – that is, printing money – could counterbalance fiscal tightening.

Until recently, the OBR, broadly in line with the IMF, assumed a fiscal multiplier of 0.6: for every dollar cut from government spending, the economy would shrink by only 60 cents. This assumes "Ricardian equivalence": debt-financed public spending at least partly crowds out private spending through its impact on expectations and confidence. If households and firms anticipate a tax increase in the future as a result of government borrowing today, they will reduce their consumption and investment accordingly.

On this view, if fiscal austerity relieves households of the burden of future tax increases, they will increase their spending. This may be true when the economy is operating at full employment – when state and market are in competition for every last resource. But when there is spare capacity in the economy, the resources "freed up" by public-sector retrenchment may simply be wasted.

Forecasting organizations are finally admitting that they underestimated the fiscal multiplier. The OBR, reviewing its recent mistakes, accepted that "the average [fiscal] multiplier over the two years would have needed to be 1.3 – more than double our estimate – to fully explain the weak level of GDP in 2011-12." The IMF has conceded that "multipliers have actually been in the 0.9 and 1.7 range since the Great Recession." The effect of underestimating the fiscal multiplier has been systematic misjudgment of the damage that "fiscal consolidation" does to the economy.

This leads us to the second mistake. Forecasters assumed that monetary expansion would provide an effective antidote to fiscal contraction. The Bank of England hoped that by printing £375 billion of new money, ($600 billion), it would stimulate total spending to the tune of £50 billion, or 3 per cent of GDP.

But the evidence emerging from successive rounds of QE in the UK and the US suggests that while it did lower bond yields, the extra money was largely retained within the banking system, and never reached the real economy. This implies that the problem has mainly been a lack of demand for credit – reluctance on the part of businesses and households to borrow on almost any terms in a flat market.

These two mistakes compounded each other: If the negative impact of austerity on economic growth is greater than was originally assumed, and the positive impact of quantitative easing is weaker, then the policy mix favored by practically all European governments has been hugely wrong. There is much greater scope for fiscal stimulus to boost growth, and much smaller scope for monetary stimulus.

This is all quite technical, but it matters a great deal for the welfare of populations. All of these models assume outcomes on the basis of existing policies. Their consistent over-optimism about these policies' impact on economic growth validates pursuing them, and enables governments to claim that their remedies are "working," when they clearly are not.

This is a cruel deception. Before they can do any good, the forecasters must go back to the drawing board, and ask themselves whether the theories of the economy underpinning their models are the right ones.

37. Meeting our Makers

New Statesman | December 18, 2012

In the early 1950s, Britain was an industrial giant. Today it is an industrial pygmy. Manufacturing was industry's bedrock. In 1952 it produced a third of national output, employed 40 per cent of the workforce, and made up a quarter of world manufacturing exports. Today manufacturing is just 12 per cent of GDP, employs only 8 per cent of the workforce, and sells 2 per cent of the world's manufacturing exports. The iconic names of industrial Britain are history: in their place is the service economy and supermarkets selling mainly imported goods. What happened? Was it inevitable? Does it matter?

Nicholas Comfort's book is exactly what its title promises: a roll call of the dead and the dying. The broad outline of the story is well-known. Britain ended the Second World War with a technological edge in aircraft, aerospace, computers, and electronics which it failed to exploit. In the 1950 and early 1960s, British manufacturers dominated the home market and had about 20 per cent of world exports, with some world beaters like the Comet airliner, the Mini, and Triumph motorbikes. Then a decline set in with increasing import penetration and declining export sales, till the trade surplus in manufactures finally disappeared in 1983.

In the 1970s many firms with household names went under. Governments, starting with Edward Heath, desperately tried to keep 'lame ducks' like Rolls Royce afloat by nationalizing them. Thatcher returned the lame ducks to 'the chill forces of the market', many of them drowning. Manufacturing went on shrinking under New Labour, with the manufacturing workforce fell from 4.5m to 2.5m between 1997 and 2010. 'Financial and business services', writes Comfort, 'were seen [by the New Labour government] as the way forward for Britain, with manufacturing recognised as globally competitive only in aerospace and pharmaceuticals'. As immigrant workers flooded into Britain's services and food processing sector, manufacturing jobs flooded out, mainly to the Far East. Flagship businesses were sold to foreign firms, notably the takeover of Cadbury's by Kraft in 2010. No story, writes Comfort, is more poignant than the 'fall of two of the giants of the 20th century British economy – GEC and ICI'.

Every advanced economy has been affected by the shift from manufacturing to services but the sheer scale of the industrial decline in Britain demands a special effort at explanation. After all, Germany has kept a much larger manufacturing capacity, and its workers work fewer hours. France, too, had maintained world class manufacturing companies like Dassault and Peugeot. Why did Britain fail to emulate them?

Unfortunately, we don't get an explanation here. Like almost every writer on industry, Comfort cannot see the wood for the trees. The reader is wearied by page after page of blunders, business miscalculations, and missed opportunities, failed grandiose projects like Concorde, firms going bust, changing their owners, changing their names, and either disappearing, or reappearing in shrunken form with new acronyms. Comfort spreads a thin coat of 'factors' to cover every possible influence: not just 'fuddy-duddy management, failure to invest, outdated working practices and head-in-the-sand trade unions' but also 'short-termism in the City and the Treasury; the sterile and destructive cycle of nationalisation and privatisation; poor decision-making by government; inadequate market size at home; an obsession with size; the transfer of jobs to the developing world; takeovers driven by boardroom egos; boardroom disdain for manufacturing as such; the lure of Wall Street; sheer bad luck – and good old-fashioned incompetence'. Some old saws – comprehensive education and health & safety legislation – are duly wheeled out to complete the list. As Churchill once said of a dessert placed before him: 'This pudding lacks a theme'.

A historian of British industry should be able to do better than this. Of course, there cannot be a single explanation of the British economic experience. But we can suggest two important ones. The first was the imperial overhang. Until well into the 1960s most British companies expected to go on earning their living from the Empire – that financial, industrial, and military complex making up the imperial system. Premonitions of industrial decline – 'Made in Germany', the 'Yellow Peril' - date from late Victorian and Edwardian times. Joseph Chamberlain's 1903 campaign for tariff reform – Protection plus imperial preference - was deliberately designed to reduce competitive pressure from Germany and Japan. It is easy to forget that for two-third of the last century competition was repelled not by superior British efficiency but by military force: it took some time after defeat in the Second World War for German and Japanese competition to start up again.

Imperial policy was not wholly consistent. Maintaining the sterling area – not finally wound up till 1977 - required high interest rates and an overvalued exchange rate which hit manufacturing. But it was part of a system of sterling loans tied to orders for British exports, a British government procurement system for imperial defence, a resource-extraction system from imperial primary producers. The British aircraft, shipbuilding, railway, motor vehicle industries were under no pressure to modernise their plant, upskill their managers and workers, or reform their archaic labour practices when they could rely on captive domestic and imperial markets. Complacency ruled; entrepreneurship was at a discount. Globalisation put a stop to all that.

After the breakdown of the imperial system, the big problem facing British industry was erratic government policy. In the 1950s, Conservative governments pursued benign neglect. Governments of the 1960s and 1970s, mainly Labour, decided that the future lay in 'industrial policy': making industries more efficient by reorganizing them. Governments would 'pick winners', as allegedly the French and Japanese did. Industrial policy started up with the National Economic Development Council and its 'little Neddies'; it gathered strength with the merger boom and nationalizations of the 1960s and 1970s; it was discredited with Tony Benn's attempt to turn collapsed industries into workers' cooperatives; it was abolished by Margaret Thatcher in 1979. Running through this history is a lack of continuity: government policy towards taxation and incentives continually changed, long-term aims were repeatedly sacrificed to short-term financial exigencies, projects were taken up and abandoned when they became too costly, fashions in thinking shifted, waste was colossal. The result was never-ending unsettlement and uncertainty. The theoretical debate which went on at this time between 'governments'and 'markets' was largely off beam. Both business and government miscalculations were equally gross.

As the former civil servant Chris Benjamin has written (in Strutting on Thin Air) 'the underlying essential for industrial success is "continuity"...continuity fosters consistent focus, expertise evolved over decades and pursuit of research, innovation and knowledge application to secure the feedback for "increasing returns"'.

But, in the end, does industrial decline matter if we can earn our living in other ways? Comfort is of the school which laments that "Britain has forgotten how to make things", but it is not easy to separate out the economics from the nostalgia in this statement. Economic policy should not be determined by misty-eyed reminiscences about the brand names of decades past, or by a nationalism derived from the tangibility of 'things'. Comfort certainly feels more at home complaining about where Terry's Chocolate Orange is now made (Poland) than explaining why an economy less reliant on services might be a healthier one. He deplores the fact that while Queen Elizabeth's coronation souvenirs were made in Britain, knick-knacks for the Diamond Jubilee were mostly made in China – as if cheap souvenirs were the secret recipe for Britain's economic future.

Yet there is more to be said. Almost the last gasp of the view that manufacturing mattered was the House of Lords Select Committee Report on Overseas Trade in 1985. It asked: what would happen to our balance of trade when surpluses from North Sea oil ran out? The then

Chancellor, Nigel Lawson, replied succinctly: services would take up the slack.

But this is a superficial response, for a number of reasons. First, insofar as the big gainer from loss of manufacturing has been financial services, it has greatly increased the tendency to short-termism. Michael Heseltine, as President of the Board of Trade in 1993, said in Parliament:

> 'I do not doubt for one moment that deep-seated short-term attitudes are prevalent in our affairs; or that this is one important strand in understanding why we as a nation have performed less well than many of our competitors. Such attitudes have led us to invest less than we might in technology and advanced means of production. They have encouraged growth in companies by acquisition and financial engineering rather than through organic development and building on products and markets. They have led us to place far too great an emphasis on comparisons of near-term financial results in judging our companies, instead of considering the strength of management and its underlying strategy. Those attitudes are of a piece'.

Second, Britain's reliance on financial services has increased the volatility of government revenue. The financial sector, as the experience of 2008 showed, is particularly prone to boom and bust. Financial volatility affects all incomes, including the income of the government. Because of its disproportionate reliance on the inflated taxes from the financial sector, the British government's revenues collapsed disproportionately when the financial sector failed. This helps explain why the our government's 'structural deficit' was greater than those of countries with more balanced economies. It had become over-reliant on a particularly volatile income stream. Like individuals, governments should hold balanced portfolios. No government should remain indifferent to the distribution and performance of a nation's assets, human or physical, because on that depends its ability to fulfil its social functions. Governments therefore need to promote a balanced economy.

Finally, services of all kinds are less good than manufacturing in securing high employment, and progressive increases in median incomes. In the long run, of course, automation is bound to reduce manufacturing employment, but as long as manufactures are such a large part of international trade, they are important for maintaining employment in a trading economy, because most services cannot be exported. A country which loses its industrial base will thus experience rising structural unemployment apart from automation.

Manufactures are also a safeguard against income deterioration because they are more productive than most services. The more people employed in labour intensive activities – especially retail services - the lower the typical income will be. The loss of two million manufacturing jobs between 1997 and 2010 probably explains why Gordon Brown, despite his best efforts, was unable to increase average productivity growth in the period.

For these reasons, Lawson's dismissal of the case for manufacturing as 'special pleading dressed up as analysis' is not the last word on the subject. It is a shame that Nicholas Comfort has missed the chance to put that case in more persuasive form.

38. Supply matters – but so does demand
Robert Skidelsky and Marcus Miller
Financial Times | February 18, 2013

At long last, the defenders of George Osborne's deficit-reduction strategy have come up with a reasoned case.

The thoughtful argument in support of the UK chancellor is made by Ryan Bourne and Tim Knox, economists at the centre-right Centre for Policy Studies think-tank. They say that Britain suffered a huge supply shock following the recession of 2008. This left it not only with reduced output, but also – by undermining the banking system and by causing a big increase in state spending and the national debt – with less capacity to produce output.

Since the problem is one of reduced capacity, Bourne and Knox contend, expansionary monetary and fiscal policy will not solve it. Policy should, instead, aim at raising the "medium term growth rate". How to achieve this? By a "relentless focus on reducing the burden of government spending", combined with measures that include cutting welfare benefits and taxes, rehabilitating the banks, scrapping planning laws and opening up public services to competition.

The logic is the familiar one that high public spending, whether financed by borrowing or taxation, crowds out more efficient private spending. So even if their recommended transfer of resources to the private sector involves a large drop in current output, these transitional costs will be worth it. Policies to avoid or mitigate this cost are wrong-headed. We would be, as Bourne and Knox say, mortgaging our future. So it is more austerity we need, not less.

Restive rightwing backbenchers from Mr Osborne's Conservative party, such as Dominic Raab and Liam Fox, who urge him to go further and faster down this road, dismiss the chancellor's insufficiently austere policy – including the fact that he has twice revised his deficit-reduction schedule – as weakness of will. Indeed, they take the increase in public spending to be the explanation (together with the collapse of the banking system) for the UK's miserable growth rate since Mr Osborne took office. Like those who blame the crutches for the patient's inability to walk normally, they would kick away the crutches.

Bourne and Knox nevertheless advise further years of belt-tightening as a price worth paying to transfer resources from public to private sector.

Apart from the dire implications for income inequality, there is a flaw in their position: it ignores the subtle connection between demand and supply. Prolonged unemployment, or underemployment, destroys not just current but also potential output. A physics graduate may be able to find employment as a cab driver or waiter. But how much physics "potential" will they retain after years of doing such jobs? Economists call this "rusting away" of human capacity through disuse "hysteresis". If an output gap is allowed to persist, the effect of hysteresis on skills and infrastructure is to reduce the growth potential of the economy itself.

Supply-siders and their Keynesian critics both agree that the government should help to protect and promote the output potential of the economy. The difference is that the supply-siders ignore demand and focus entirely on direct measures to improve economic efficiency, as listed above. By contrast, modern followers of John Maynard Keynes, both in this country and in the US, believe that an essential element of a growth strategy is to avoid a prolonged recession by acting directly to maintain demand.

We touch here on the oldest debate in macroeconomics. Early in the 19th century, the French economist Jean-Baptiste Say proclaimed: "Supply creates its own demand." There could never be a shortage of demand, he said, because people necessarily spend what they earn, either on consumption or investment. But, in the conditions of the 1930s Great Depression, Keynes pointed out the fault in this logic. Money earned is not necessarily spent: part of it is saved, and savings may be held in cash. Indeed, the lower people's confidence in the future, the more of their savings they will want to hold in cash. So demand can fall below supply.

With skills (or "human capital") recognised as a factor of production, we can transcend this age-old division between supply-siders and demand-siders. Because of hysteresis, pure supply-side policies are not sufficient. Buoyant demand, though necessary for sustained medium-term growth, is not sufficient either: supply-friendly policies are also called for. As the recent London School of Economics Growth Commission report points out, the promotion of skills, the development of infrastructure and support for innovation are "the essential drivers of the productivity growth on which the UK's future prosperity depends".

In present conditions of depressed demand, the provision of more skills and better infrastructure in Britain is not a call for more mindless austerity. It is a call for productive investment by both government and private sector to create jobs today and to promote growth in the future. Surely we can all agree on that?

Marcus Miller is professor of economics at the University of Warwick

39. Austere Illusions
Project Syndicate | May 21, 2013

The doctrine of imposing present pain for future benefit has a long history – stretching all the way back to Adam Smith and his praise of "parsimony." It is particularly vociferous in "hard times." In 1930, US President Herbert Hoover was advised by his treasury secretary, Andrew Mellon: "Liquidate labor, liquidate stocks, liquidate the farmers, liquidate real estate. It will purge the rottenness out of the system...People will...live a more moral life...and enterprising people will pick up the wrecks from less competent people."

To "liquidationists" of Mellon's ilk, the pre-2008 economy was full of cancerous growths – in banking, in housing, in equities – which need to be cut out before health can be restored. Their position is clear: the state is a parasite, sucking the lifeblood of free enterprise. Economies gravitate naturally to a full-employment equilibrium, and, after a shock, do so fairly quickly if not impeded by misguided government action. This is why they are fierce opponents of Keynesian interventionism.

Keynes's heresy was to deny that there are any such natural forces, at least in the short term. This was the point of his famous remark, "In the long run we are all dead." Economies, Keynes believed, can become stuck in prolonged periods of "under-employment equilibrium"; in such cases, an external stimulus of some kind is needed to jolt them back to higher employment.

Simply put, Keynes believed that we cannot all cut our way to growth at the same time. To believe otherwise is to commit the "fallacy of composition." What is true of the parts is not true of the whole. If all of Europe is cutting, the United Kingdom cannot grow; if the entire world is cutting, global growth will stop.

In these circumstances, austerity is exactly the opposite of what is needed. A government cannot liquidate its deficit if the source of its revenues, the national income, is diminishing. It is deficit reduction, not debt, that is profligate, because it implies wastage of available human and physical capital, quite apart from the resulting misery.

Austerity's advocates rely on one – and only one – argument: If fiscal contraction is part of a credible "consolidation" program aimed at permanently reducing the share of government in GDP, business expectations will be so encouraged by the prospect of lower taxes and higher profits that the resulting economic expansion will more than offset the contraction in demand caused by cuts in public spending. The economist Paul Krugman calls this the "confidence fairy."

The pro-austerity argument is pure assertion, but it is meant to be a testable assertion, so econometricians have been busy trying to prove that the less the government spends, the faster the economy will grow. Indeed, just a year or two ago, "expansionary fiscal contraction" was all the rage, and a massive research effort went into proving its existence.

Economists arrived at some striking correlations. For example, "an increase in government size by ten percentage points is associated with a 0.5-1 per cent lower annual growth rate." In April 2010, the leader of this school, Harvard University's Alberto Alesina, assured European finance ministers that "even sharp reductions of budget deficits have been accompanied and immediately followed by sustained growth rather than recessions even in the very short run."

But two fallacies vitiated the "proofs" offered by Alesina and others. First, because the cuts had to be "credible" – that is, large and decisive – the continuing absence of growth could be blamed on the insufficiency of the cuts. Thus, Europe's failure to recover "immediately" has been due to a lack of austerity, even though public-sector retrenchment has been unprecedented.

Second, the researchers committed the arch-statistical mistake of confusing correlation with causation. If you find a correlation between deficit reduction and growth, the reduction could be causing the growth or vice versa. (Or both the deficit reduction and the growth could be due to something else – devaluation or higher exports, for example.)

An International Monetary Fund paper in 2012 brought Alesina's hour of glory to an end. Going through the same material as Alesina had, its authors pointed out that "while it is plausible to conjecture that confidence effects have been at play in our sample of consolidations, during downturns they do not seem to have ever been strong enough to make the consolidations expansionary." Fiscal contraction is contractionary, period.

An even more spectacular example of a statistical error and sleight of hand is the widely cited claim of Harvard economists Carmen Reinhart and Kenneth Rogoff that countries' growth slows sharply if their debt/GDP ratio exceeds 90 per cent. This finding reflected the massive overweighting of one country in their sample, and there was the same confusion between correlation and causation seen in Alesina's work: high debt levels may cause a lack of growth, or a lack of growth may cause high debt levels.

On this foundation of zombie economics and slipshod research rests the case for austerity. In fact, the austerity boosters in the UK and Europe frequently cited the Alesina and Reinhart/Rogoff findings.

The results of austerity have been what any Keynesian would have expected: hardly any growth in the UK and the eurozone in the last two and a half years, and huge declines in some countries; little reduction in public deficits, despite large spending cuts; and higher national debts.

Two other consequences of austerity are less appreciated. First, prolonged unemployment destroys not just current but also potential output by eroding the "human capital" of the unemployed. Second, austerity policies have hit those at the bottom of the income distribution far more severely than those at the top, simply because those at the top rely much less on government services.

So we will remain in a state of "under-employment equilibrium" until policy in the UK and the eurozone is changed (and assuming that policy in the US does not become worse). In the face of clamour from the right to cut even more savagely, statesmen who are too timid to increase public spending would be wise to ignore their advice.

40. Economic Rebalancing
Project Syndicate | May 21, 2013

We all know how the global economic crisis began. The banks over-lent to the housing market. The subsequent burst of the housing bubble in the United States caused banks to fail, because banking had gone global and the big banks held one another's bad loans. Banking failure caused a credit crunch. Lending dried up and economies started shrinking.

So governments bailed out banks and economies, producing a sovereign debt crisis. With everyone busy deleveraging, economies failed to recover. Much of the world, especially Europe, but also the slightly less sickly US, remains stuck in a semi-slump.

So how do we escape from this hole? The familiar debate is between austerity and stimulus. "Austerians" believe that only balancing government budgets and shrinking national debts will restore investor confidence. The Keynesians believe that without a large fiscal stimulus – a deliberate temporary increase of the deficit – the European and US economies will remain stuck in recession for years to come.

I am one of those who believe that recovery from the crisis requires fiscal stimulus. I don't think monetary policy, even unorthodox monetary policy, can do the job. Confidence is too low for commercial banks to create credit on the scale needed to return to full employment and the pre-crisis growth trend, however many hundreds of billions of whatever cash central banks pour into them. We are learning all over again that the central bank cannot create whatever level of credit it wants!

So, like Paul Krugman, Martin Wolf, and others, I would expand fiscal deficits, not try to shrink them. I advocate this for the old-fashioned Keynesian reason that we are suffering from a deficiency of aggregate demand, that the multiplier is positive, and that the most effective way to reduce the private and public debts a year or two down the line is by taking steps to boost growth in national income now.

But the argument between austerians and Keynesians over how to encourage sustained recovery intersects with another debate. Simply put, what kind of post-recovery economy do we want? This is where economics becomes political economy.

Those who believe that all was fine with the pre-crisis economy except for banks making crazy loans are convinced that preventing such crises in the future requires only banking reform. The new reform orthodoxy is "macro-prudential regulation" of commercial banks by the central bank. Some would go further and either nationalize the banks or break them up. But their horizon of reform is similarly confined to the banking sector, and they rarely ask what caused the banks to behave so badly.

In fact, it is possible to regard excessive bank lending as a symptom of deeper economic flaws. The economist Thomas Palley sees it as a means of offsetting growth in income inequality, with access to cheap credit replacing the broken welfare guarantee of social democracy. So reform requires redistribution of wealth and incomes.

Redistributive measures go quite well with stimulus policies, because they may be expected to increase aggregate demand in the short term (owing to lower-income households' higher propensity to consume) and minimize the economy's dependence on debt financing in the long term. Initial damage to the confidence of the business class caused by higher taxes on the wealthy would be balanced by the prospect of higher overall consumption.

Others argue that we should try to rebalance the economy not just from rich to poor, but also from energy-wasting to energy-saving. The premise of the green economic agenda is that we have reached the ecological limits of our current growth model, and that we will need to find ways of living that reduce demands on non-renewable sources of energy.

So stimulus policies should aim to stimulate not just demand per se; they must focus, instead, on stimulating ecologically-friendly demand. For example, greens advocate free municipal transport in major cities. In general, they argue, we need more care, not more cars, so stimulus money should go to health, education, and the protection of the environment.

The truth is that any fiscally-driven recovery policy is bound to have reformist implications. That is why the austerians are so against it, and why even those who accept the theoretical case for a stimulus insist on implementing it through monetary policy alone.

Re-balancing the economy from gas-guzzling to energy-saving – and from private to public consumption – is bound to alter the goal of economic policy. Maximizing GDP growth will no longer be the top priority; rather, it should be something we might want to call "happiness," or "well-being," or the "good life."

The radical case is that the pre-crisis economy crashed not because of preventable mistakes in banking, but because money had become the sole arbiter of value. So we should be energetic in seeking recovery, but not in a way that simply reproduces the structural flaws of the past.

As Dani Rodrik has well put it: "If economics were only about profit maximization, it would be just another name for business administration. It is a social discipline, and society has other means of cost accounting beside market prices."

41. Economic Prosperity Debate
House of Lords | July 18, 2013

[Bracketed sections were omitted in the delivered speech due to time limits]

My Lords, I am grateful to the noble Lord, Lord Haskel, for introducing this important discussion. He has been rightly impressed by the argument put forward by the noble Lord, Lord Sainsbury, that the state must play a key part in fostering innovation, and I agree with that. However, of course, that does not exhaust the role of the state in creating prosperity. In the last chapter of his General Theory, the economist Keynes pinpointed as,

> "The outstanding faults of the ... society in which we live ... its failure to provide for full employment and its arbitrary and inequitable distribution of wealth and incomes".

I believe that these are still the outstanding faults of the society in which we live and that the state has a vital role to play in remedying them. Moreover, that is clearly connected to the topic of the noble Lord, Lord Haskel. The worst environment for innovation is rampant economic insecurity and excessive inequality. The private sector will not invest in jobs and skills unless it sees a market. The state has a role to play in sustaining that market in general, as well as in providing support to particular sectors. Once again I apologise for being the only macroeconomist taking part in this debate—I feel very lonely.

Let us consider two arguments. After the Thatcher-Reagan revolution, politicians and economists no longer believed that government policy should aim directly to influence the level of employment. Noble Lords will remember the new doctrine announced by the noble Lord, Lord Lawson: government should concentrate on controlling inflation and leave employment to the market. Let us see how well the market has done. Between 1950 and 1973—the period when economic policy was influenced by the Keynes doctrine—UK unemployment averaged below 3 per cent. Since 1979, when the Lawson doctrine held sway, the average has been almost 8 per cent. Today, Britain's unemployment rate of 7.8 per cent tells only half the story. The widest indicator of joblessness, which includes unemployment, part-timers seeking full-time work and those who are economically inactive but who nevertheless want a job, is estimated at about 12 per cent, or 6.4 million people. On top of that you have to add the much higher level of youth unemployment. The Prime Minister and the Chancellor constantly tell us that the nation must live within its means and that the Government cannot spend more money than they have. Has it occurred to these great thinkers that our means include those unused resources and that if they were being properly utilised, the Government would have more money to spend?

[So as against the Lawson doctrine, I would counterpose the doctrine that the government should so manage the economy as to keep unemployment stable at between 5 per cent and 6 per cent; and insofar as it fails, it should be prepared to act as employer of the last resort. Had it acted on these principles after 2008 we would have had less pain and faster recovery.]

The second revolution that has been associated with Lady Thatcher was the abandonment of any commitment to equality. The ideology of the 1980s was that undue compression of incomes brought about stagnation: get taxes and welfare benefits down in order to increase the incentives to work and innovate and the result would be a more dynamic economy and one in which wealth would steadily trickle down without any need for obvious redistributionary policies. The trade-off has not happened—growth was slower than it was in the Keynesian period and we are waiting for the trickle-down to happen. In the past 30 years, the share of income captured by the top 1 per cent has more than doubled to 14 per cent, leading to the joke that the new class struggle is between the have-nots and the have-yachts.

[The Gini index, which measures inequality, increased from 26 in the 1970s to 36, its highest level in more than half a century, by 2008]

The economist Tony Atkinson, the great expert on distribution, writes:

"Moves towards reduced income inequality were dramatically reversed in the 1980s with a sharp rise in inequality",

a rise which was historically unprecedented. Margaret Thatcher and her successors—we should note this historical fact—dismantled two of the main drivers of equalisation: the system of progressive taxation, and strong trade unions. The old tax system set, in effect, a cap on post-tax incomes and profits. The call for caps on bankers' remuneration today simply reflects the failure of the current tax system to limit its stratospheric rise. The main achievement of the trade unions was to push up pre-tax earnings in line with productivity. This function has now collapsed.

The triumph of greed over professionalism and restraint has been most obvious in the financial services sector, which, ironically, new Labour decided was to become the powerhouse of the British economy. I understand well the frustration of the noble Lord, Lord Sainsbury of Turville—as a Minister for Science and Innovation under new Labour, he was told that the financial services were a great source of innovation. When he asked for examples he was told that,

"tax avoidance is an art where we are very innovative".

[Any policy to lift us permanently out of slump conditions needs to deal with the issue of income distribution. In the short-run, stimulus money should go towards those with the highest marginal propensity to spend –for example, any tax cuts should be targeted at the poor, the reverse of the welfare cuts now in train.

In the longer-run we need more post-tax equality in order to stabilise the broad base of consumption and free it from its excessive reliance on debt.

Further, the government should steps through minimum wage legislation to raise the pre-tax incomes of the lowest paid]

I have no doubt that we will recover from the present semi-slump; we may even recover sufficiently by 2015 to give the coalition—or the Conservatives at least—another term of office. My great fear is that, having got to something like normal, we will come to believe that we can continue much as before, except for a few watered-down reforms to the banks. I believe, on the contrary, that the system of political economy that has evolved since the 1980s has, for all its benefits, grave flaws that, if allowed to continue uncorrected, will land us in a succession of crashes and crises of differing degrees of severity, which will cumulatively destroy support for the free-market economy. The chief of these flaws in our system are, to repeat Keynes,

"its failure to provide for full employment and its arbitrary and inequitable distribution of wealth and incomes".

The Government have a big role to play in addressing both. I am grateful to the noble Lord, Lord Haskel, for giving me the chance to set out my ideas on these matters.

VII. GREEN SHOOTS AT LAST?

42. Labour should hammer home one simple message on the economy

The Guardian | August 13, 2013

The Labour party faces a political dilemma. Barely a day goes past without the more excitable parts of the British press trumpeting some new signal of Britain's economic success. Every other headline screams that Britain is "booming" or that its factories are "roaring to life". Every little jump in the flimsiest of economic indicators, every upward revision of economic forecasts, is celebrated as if it were a triumph worthy of song. And the propaganda seems to be working: voters' confidence in Conservative economic management has soared, and in Labour's has slumped.

So how should Labour respond? The first requirement is to separate the politics from the facts. Britain is not booming. Growth is forecast to be 1.2 per cent this year – a dismal performance by any historical standard. As the Bank of England governor, Mark Carney, said in his first press conference: "This remains the slowest recovery in output on record."

Five years after the onset of the financial crisis, Britain's economy is still 3.5 per cent smaller than it was in 2008. Growth may have spurted ahead of Britain's competitors in the last quarter, but this comparison neglects the fact that it suffered a bigger fall in output and experienced a weaker recovery. The US, Germany and even France have surpassed their pre-recession peaks. Even according to the brightest forecasts, we will need another two years to make up the lost ground. And the picture is worse when we factor in population growth; GDP per capita is not expected to reach its pre-recession peak until 2018. We are only halfway through a lost decade.

The second task is to point out the brittleness of the recovery. Despite the government's rhetoric on "rebalancing", the growth strategy on which it relies is to reinflate the same bubble that caused the crisis in the first place. That is the real meaning, and effect, of quantitative easing.

The recovery, such as it is, is disproportionately based on debt-fuelled consumer spending and inflated house prices. This approach has been entrenched in government policy with the Funding for Lending and Help to Buy schemes, which channel money into the dysfunctional housing market. Even the housebuilders who will benefit from Help to Buy have warned that it could be "very dangerous" for the economy. When real wages have fallen by 5.5 per cent in the past three years, and with the household saving ratio at rock bottom, the insistent question should be: how long can such a narrow recovery last?

The opposition has not figured out how to react to the "good news". It was easy enough to point out Chancellor George Osborne's failures when the economy was flatlining. Ed Balls, the shadow chancellor, made promising, if inconsistent, efforts to offer an economic alternative. True, too often Labour's critique lacked any theoretical bite. It preferred to repeat that Osborne's cuts were "too far, too fast", rather than explaining why the cuts would harm the economy. But at the first sign of any economic growth, Labour has swallowed its tongue. Its focus on falling living standards targets the symptoms of an unhealthy economy, rather than the cause. Its decision to blame immigration for Britain's ills, a tactic dusted off from the Blair years, is economically illiterate.

The truth is that Labour is terrified that the perception of economic recovery – the "feelgood factor" – may count for more than the facts of a recovery that leaves 8 per cent unemployed, five job applications for each vacancy, falling living standards, thousands of ruined businesses, and millions of part-time, minimum wage, zero-hours contract jobs.

It fears that, set against the gloom of the past three years, the enthusiasm produced by even a low level of growth may be enough to keep the government, or at least the Conservatives, in power. This argument has a long pedigree: Ed Miliband has no desire to be another Neil Kinnock, proclaiming doom when things are palpably improving.

The politics of the matter is far from simple. But if I were in Labour's shoes I would hammer home one simple message: the pain has not been worth it because the recovery is not secure. I would explain why printing money to offset cuts in public spending is the flakiest possible route to growth and is bound to land us in a fresh crisis sooner rather than later, and why an alternative policy of targeting growth and letting the deficit look after itself would be better for growth and for the debt. And I would have enough confidence in my argument to wait for events to vindicate it, rather than flopping around with each new set of figures.

43. The folly of George Osborne: Growth is good – but the point of it is to make us feel better, and we don't
The Independent | October 25, 2013

The Chancellor has been celebrating the recent estimates showing that the economy has grown by 0.8 per cent in the third quarter of this year. However, these forecasts do not tell us anything about what is most important: well-being. National well-being is the only object of economic growth, but GDP data says nothing about it.

Well-being depends on a range of factors, including amount of leisure time, good health, security of income, sense of community, a clean environment, harmony with nature, respect for personality, and so on. It also includes sustainability of the ecological basis of human life. Either these things do not show up in GDP at all, or turn up as subtractions from GDP growth. For example, the more medicines people consume, the more hours they work, and the more polluted the atmosphere – the higher the GDP!

The latest estimates do not settle the debate of how the economy might have fared under an alternative strategy either. Critics of Osborne's policies never claimed that the economy would not recover from the collapse of 2008-2009. Economies always recover from their low points, whatever the policies pursued, sooner or later. The real question is whether the recovery was delayed by austerity and whether it could have been stronger without austerity.

So first, what do the latest results by the ONS say? In summary, the economy has grown by 0.8 per cent in the third quarter of this year, up from 0.7 in the last quarter and up by 1.5 per cent compared to Q3 2012. This is the fastest growth in three years. It is somewhat more broadly-based than last quarter's. But the economy is still 2.5 per cent below its peak in 2008. Most of the growth has been in the housing sector, with construction boosted by the Government's "Help to Buy" scheme. Production output is still 12.5 per cent down.

Osborne tweeted "Britain's hard work is paying off", but has the hard slog really been worth it? Not necessarily. Most economists agree that the Chancellor's austerity policy has inflicted significant damage on the economy, quite apart from the damage caused by the recession itself.

Economists Alan Taylor and Òscar Jordà even estimated that each year of Osborne knocked 1 per cent off growth, meaning that UK GDP would be 3 per cent higher today without austerity. This corresponds to £92bn all told, enough to restore Labour's school-building plans and still have enough change to plug the funding gap in the NHS. For the average household, this amounts to a loss of £3,500 over three years – and, as Taylor and Jordà point out, this is a conservative estimate.

In other words, we might have had the recovery sooner, without having had to pay the cost of three years of output foregone. And the growth potential of the economy might well have been greater had the unemployed been absorbed into production sooner, instead of their skills being allowed to rust away.

In particular, the UK could have secured itself a brighter recovery by investing extensively in infrastructure, without having to add a single penny to the deficit. Economic analysis suggests that every £1 spent in construction returns £2.84 to the economy. Through this multiplier effect, construction could have offered a route out of recession.

The economy has turned a corner, and this is to be welcomed. But we should not imagine the game is won. Osborne's satisfaction is like that of a football team which scores its first goal, forgetting it is 3 nil down.

The question, of course, is whether the recovery, in the jargon, is "sustainable", or whether it will peter out before full health is restored. This depends partly on the level of aggregate demand, or spending, both in the UK and abroad. From the findings of Taylor and Jordà, households have £3,500 less to spend than in 2008. The recovery will have to do a lot of hard lifting to raise the total level of spending to what it was before. A housing-cum-construction boom on its own will not be enough.

The depreciation of the pound has helped our exports, but the eurozone remains flat, and the IMF has recently reduced its 2014 growth estimates for the big emerging economies like China, India, and Brazil, to whom the eurosceptics say we should direct our exports.

However, sustainability also depends on the long-term balance of the economy: not just how much is produced, but what is produced, and to whom it goes. The pre-recession economy relied disproportionately on the growth of the financial sector; and that meant that rewards to financial activities – from the activity of buying and selling existing assets – grew much faster than rewards to producers of actual goods and services. This has become scandalous. The UK mean income in 2011 was £27,000, but the median income was £21,500. That means that 50 per cent of people earned less than £27,000; and 12 million people were officially "in poverty" – defined as having less than half of the median income. One cannot say whether the welfare of a country's citizens is going up or down without knowing what has happened to income distribution.

The recovery so far promises to perpetuate this imbalance. Specifically, the extension of "Help to Buy" to existing houses will boost house prices with minimal encouragement for the construction of new houses. And quantitative easing – the only stimulus policy the Government finds acceptable – tends in the same direction by increasing the wealth of those who have assets to trade. In other words, the current pattern of recovery does nothing to counter the growth of income inequality, which was, arguably, the main cause of the crash of 2008, and actually makes it worse. "To those who own, it shall be given."

Hindering the emergence of a broader conception of sustainability is our continual obsession with GDP growth. Gross Domestic Product is undeniably an important indicator of a country's economic health. It is the most important economic statistic in the short term. However, because it only measures that portion of domestic production traded in markets, it fails to capture the growth of well-being, the only rational reason for economic growth.

The argument for a wider measure than GDP is strengthened by empirical evidence of the lack of a close fit between GDP growth and subjective wellbeing. A recent ONS report shows that, although London is the fastest growing region of the UK, it has the lowest average rating for life satisfaction and the highest average rating for anxiety in the UK. To the extent that GDP is therefore not synonymous with welfare, policy for sustainability should concentrate on the growth of the requirements for well-being rather than on the growth of GDP. Economic growth would have to be viewed as a residual rather than something that policy must be aimed at. David Cameron perhaps had something of this in mind in his initial talk of the "big society". It is time to revive the language, and match it by deeds.

44. Misconceiving British Austerity
Project Syndicate | October 21, 2013

Was the British government's decision to embrace austerity in the wake of the global financial crisis the right policy, after all? Yes, claims the economist Kenneth Rogoff in a much-discussed recent commentary. Rogoff argues that while, in hindsight, the government should have borrowed more, at the time there was a real danger that Britain would go the way of Greece. So Chancellor of the Exchequer George Osborne turns out, on this view, to be a hero of global finance.

To show that there was a real threat of capital flight, Rogoff uses historical cases to demonstrate that the United Kingdom's credit performance has been far from credible. He mentions the 1932 default on its World War I debt owed to the United States, the debts accumulated after World War II, and the UK's "serial dependence on International Monetary Fund bailouts from the mid-1950s until the mid-1970s."

What Rogoff's analysis lacks is the context in which these supposed offenses were committed. The 1932 default on Britain's WWI loans from America remains the largest blemish on the UK's debt history, but the background is crucial. The world emerged from the Great War in the shadow of a mountain of debt that the victorious Allies owed to one another (the US being the only net creditor), and by the losers to the victors. John Maynard Keynes predicted accurately that all of these debts would end up in default.

The UK was the only country that made an effort to pay. Having failed to collect what other countries owed it, Britain continued to pay the US for ten years, suspending debt service only in the depth of the Great Depression.

Rogoff's discussion about the debts accumulated after WWII is beside the point. It is neither here nor there to claim that "had the UK not used a labyrinth of rules and regulations to hold nominal interest rates on debt below inflation, its debt-to-GDP ratio might have risen over the period 1945-1955 instead of falling dramatically." The fact is that the UK did manage to reduce its debt using a series of policies, including encouragement of economic growth.

As for the UK's "serial dependence" on the IMF from the mid-1950s to the mid-1970s, there were actually only two episodes: the 1956 bailout during the Suez crisis and the 1976 bailout that preceded the winter of discontent when strikes in many essential industries – even the dead went unburied – practically brought the country to its knees. (It hardly needs stating that borrowing money from the IMF is not a default.)

In 1956, the UK was facing a speculative attack in the midst of the Suez crisis. The country was running a current-account surplus, but the pound was slipping against the dollar, causing the Bank of England to sell its dollar reserves to defend the fixed exchange rate. As its reserves drained away, Prime Minister Anthony Eden was forced to appeal for help, first to the US and then to the IMF.

The IMF's involvement was necessitated only by America's unwillingness to provide support. Furthermore, US President Dwight Eisenhower went so far as to use America's clout within the IMF to force Eden to withdraw British troops from Egypt in exchange for the loan.

The reality of the 1976 bailout is even more complicated. In the aftermath of the crisis, Chancellor of the Exchequer Denis Healey revealed that the Public Sector Borrowing Requirement had been grossly overestimated in the 1970s, and that, had he had the right figures, the UK would never have needed a loan. According to him, the Treasury even failed to recognize that the UK would have a tax surplus.

Of course, all of this had drastic implications for the economy. Tony Benn, a Labour cabinet minister in the 1970s, later revealed that the "winter of discontent," which ushered in a Tory government at the end of the decade, had been caused by the severe cuts in public expenditure demanded by the IMF: "Why did we have the winter of discontent? Because in 1976, the IMF said to the cabinet, 'You cut four billion pounds off your public expenditure or we will destroy the value of the pound sterling.'"

There is little evidence for Rogoff's implicit assumption that investors' decisions today are driven by the government's handling of its debt in the past. The number of defaults is largely irrelevant when it comes to a country like the UK, which is politically stable, carries significant economic weight, and has an independent central bank.

Consider Germany, the "biggest debt transgressor of the twentieth century," according to the economic historian Albrecht Ritschl. In the table on page 99 of their book This Time is Different, Rogoff and his co-author, Carmen Reinhart, show that Germany experienced eight debt defaults and/or restructurings from 1800 to 2008. There were also the two defaults through inflation in 1920 and 1923. And yet today Germany is Europe's economic hegemon, laying down the law to miscreants like Greece.

The truth is that a country's past failures do not influence investors if its current institutions and economic policies are sound. That was clearly the case when Osborne and his colleagues opted for austerity.

45. Shale Gas to the Rescue?
Project Syndicate | December 20, 2013

The developed world is slowly emerging from the Great Recession, but a question lingers: How fast and how far will the recovery go? One big source of pessimism has been the idea that we are running out of investment opportunities – and have been since before the 2008 crash. But is that true?

The last big surge of innovation was the Internet revolution, whose products came onstream in the 1990s. Following the dot.com collapse of the early 2000s, speculation in real estate and financial assets – enabled by cheap money – kept Western economies going. The post-2008 slump merely exposed the unsoundness of the preceding boom; the mediocrity of the recovery reflects the mediocrity of previous prospects, coolly considered. The risk now is that a debt-fueled asset spike merely perpetuates the boom-bust cycle.

The economist Larry Summers has reintroduced the term "secular stagnation" to describe what awaits us. By the mid-2000s, Summers argued at a recent International Monetary Fund conference, the average prospective return on new investment in the United States had fallen below any feasible reduction in the Federal Reserves benchmark interest rate.

That remains true today. We may be in a permanent liquidity trap, in which nominal interest rates cannot fall below zero, but the expected rate of return to investment remains negative. Unconventional monetary policies like quantitative easing may inflate a new generation of asset bubbles, but the underlying problem – negative returns to new investment – will not have been solved when the next crash comes.

So the problem is poor investment prospects. Why? In the 1930s, the economist Alvin Hansen argued that opportunities for new investment in already-rich countries were drying up. Investment growth had depended on population growth, technological innovation, and westward expansion.

With the closing of the frontier and static populations, growth would depend on innovation; but future innovation would require smaller inputs of capital and labor than in the past. In other words, the returns to capital were bound to fall as it became more abundant relative to population. In this situation, full employment could be maintained only by running continuous fiscal deficits.

John Maynard Keynes held a different view. In 1945, he wrote to T.S. Eliot: "[T]he full employment policy by means of investment is only one particular application of an intellectual theorem. You can produce the result just as well by consuming more or working less.

Personally, I regard the investment policy as first aid... Less work is the ultimate solution."

Developed countries' strong postwar investment performance dispelled fear of secular stagnation. But this occurred after a world war that had created huge pent-up demand for new equipment, transport infrastructure, and household appliances, together with a military-industrial complex that armed the West during the Cold War.

The real rate of return to capital may have started to decline by the early 1970s; productivity growth certainly has slowed since then. Some crucial changes in the political economy of Western capitalism in the 1980s can also be viewed in this light: the rise of neoliberal ideology, the growing inequality of wealth and incomes, the increase in structural unemployment, the growth of financial services, globalization, the invention of post-Cold War threats to sustain military spending, and so on.

The question today is whether a new upsurge of investment will come to our rescue. Optimists point to the shale-gas revolution in the US.

From 2005 to 2010, the US shale-gas industry's output grew at an average annual rate of 45 per cent, with the pace accelerating in 2007. As a result, shale gas accounted for nearly 40 per cent America's overall gas production in 2013 up from just 4 per cent in 2005. With the share of imports in US natural-gas consumption dropping from 16.5 per cent in 2007 to 11 per cent in 2010, America is on the path to energy self-sufficiency.

The McKinsey Global Institute has identified shale gas as a "game changer" for the world economy, estimating that it could boost America's GDP by as much as 4 per cent ($690 billion) per year and contribute an extra 1.7 million permanent jobs to the labor market by 2020. Likewise, a September 2013 report by the IHS concludes that the manufacturing, chemical and other downstream industries are also receiving a massive stimulus. "Overall, $216 billion will be invested in downstream activities like manufacturing and midstream activities like transportation from 2012-2025 as a result of shale." In 2012, out of a total of 2.1 million jobs generated in the US, nearly 377,000 jobs were created in these areas.

Beyond this, the most dramatic impact of shale gas on the economy has been the fall in energy prices. In the US, the price of natural gas has fallen to $4 MMBtu, from $13 in 2008, boosting household purchasing power. The IHS estimates that in 2012, developments in the shale-gas industry increased households' real disposable income by more than $1200. Thus the shale-gas revolution represents a huge stimulus for America, both in terms of investment, exports, and a reduction in energy costs.

I am not in a position either to judge the quantitative impact of shale gas on the US economy and, via growth there, on the rest of the world, or to comment on its geopolitical consequences or net effect on carbon emissions. But it does seem to me that contemporary apostles of secular stagnation like Summers and Paul Krugman at least ought to be taking the shale-gas revolution into account.

Index

Lightning Source UK Ltd.
Milton Keynes UK
UKOW03f0234100114

224324UK00003B/123/P